T0128815

Being Tossed *To* and *Fro?*

The Way to Steady Yourself

Evangelism and Teaching in a Two-in-One Book

M. C. PAUL

WESTBOW
P R E S S®
A DIVISION OF THOMAS NELSON
& ZONDERVAN

WestBow Press books may be ordered through booksellers or by contacting:

WestBow Press
A Division of Thomas Nelson & Zondervan
1663 Liberty Drive
Bloomington, IN 47403
www.westbowpress.com
1 (866) 928-1240

ISBN: 978-1-4908-0989-2 (sc)
ISBN: 978-1-4908-0988-5 (e)

Library of Congress Control Number: 2013917392

Print information available on the last page.

WestBow Press rev. date: 07/18/2016

TABLE OF CONTENTS

ACKNOWLEDGEMENTS

It gives me great joy to realise that I have written a book which can be of use in His service. I am grateful to my parents Late Bala Sundaram Mangam and Agnesamma who brought me up as a free and sociable child. My Sunday-school days are of much meaning to me, now. I see the hand of all-encompassing God in bringing out this book. Several years have elapsed since I engaged myself to prepare this work. All these years have been greatly rewarding in making me more and more focussed on the material that is presented. I acknowledge with gratitude the services of the Bible teachers, especially Rev. Dr. John R. W. Stott, whose books I have studied with great hunger. I use the New International Version of the Bible and the New Bible Dictionary for my study and preparation for preaching.

I thank my younger son John Stephen Mangam, Software Engineer, for his perseverance in supporting and encouraging me to write this book. He sees far ahead of me the role of this book in its usefulness to the present and future generations. I thank Miss Jyothi Raavi for her patient typing and retyping. I thank Prof. Samuel Banerjee Pallapati, my former colleague, for his help in proof-reading, advice and his good wishes for its publication. My thanks are due to Rev. Thomas Thomas, Birmingham, UK a friend of our family, for his thorough reading of the manuscript and for his invaluable suggestions in organizing the contents. God's provision is specifically seen in the support I received from my wife Suguna. She enabled me to undertake my innumerable preaching assignments, looking after children at home. These assignments consolidated my understanding of Christian truth. My other children Tabitha and Isaac have great regard for my learning which enabled me to endure my lean periods. I thank them. My thanks are due to our good friends Bob and Carol, Hyderabad, evangelists from England who have taken pains to give finishing touches to the manuscript to see it to the press. I would like to thank Sarah Davis, Kathy Lester, Susan G. and all the staff of West Bow Press, a division of Thomas Nelson for their valuable publishing and distribution services. Thank you.

M. C. Paul

Email: paulcmgm@yahoo.co.in
Mobile: +91-9440039270
Address: #21-244/1,
Noble Colony,
Machilipatnam – 521001
Andhra Pradesh – India

PREFACE

E ver since my conversion in 1969, I have great longing for studying the Bible, as a whole. I have always looked for study material for a deeper understanding. Much of my time had been spent on learning Christian doctrine from doctrinal sessions in camps and conferences of Union of Evangelical Students of India. God has provided me with an opportunity to preach many years among student groups. These years have led me to consolidate my learning. God has granted me years of interaction with the leaders of many Churches, Fellowships and Assemblies during my preaching ministry. All along 'sound doctrine' which I had assimilated has been my touchstone to test their teachings. In so doing I have become very much sensitive to notice false teaching. I have never minced words to pinpoint such false teaching. When I have pinpointed these, they have seen that it is God's word which is condemning false teaching. Perhaps, my commitment to expository preaching has been making them and me feel less uncomfortable. I know for sure that I need to speak the truth in love. If I don't do this I cannot represent our Master who is full of grace and truth. Hence I am learning to depend more and more on the Holy Spirit to be able to do this.

This book is my humble effort to help people come to true faith and to walk steadily in it. The by-product, I am sure, is going to be the correction which amateurs, who are making early steps in their false teaching, receive. I hope they are going to be the curious readers to peep into my book. Paul gives a chance for them to retract. He asks Titus, 'Warn a divisive person once, and then warn him a second time. After that, have nothing to do with him.' (Tit. 3:10). All of us make mistakes in one area or another. But it is dangerous to tread upon the area of false teaching. The earlier we backtrack the better it would be for us. The Lord is patient with us. Let us fix our eyes on Jesus. He is the author and perfecter of our faith.

SECTION I

'The all' at your yes
How it all begins

You have come of age. You are able to think for yourself. How beautiful such age is! How wonderful you look to yourself! You are brimming with self-confidence. This is exactly the time when some questions confront you as they do to all others, one day or another. These are: What are all these around me - the sun, the moon, the stars, the vegetation, the animal life…?; Where have I come from?; Where am I going?; What is life?; What is death?; Who am I after all? Before you think long enough - as though someone had told you, "don't worry, keep going" - you take a few steps. You hesitate but he tells you again: "run, run, run it's a mad, mad, mad world." Is he not telling you that it is good to be an escapist? Aren't these questions important in life? Does not an intelligent mind love to tackle these questions? If these are of importance in human life who could be behind such questions? If there is another one holding you back from facing such basic questions in life who is he? Before you think long enough, you tend to give an evasive answer. "After all I am one among a multitude of people", you say and "why bother?" is your natural response. Is it not exactly what the 'enemy' wants? Among the multitude of people there is this grand slogan - "you are free; do your own thing; let no one bother you." In the name of freedom, are they not saying 'fall in line with us', 'let us all sail together'? Where is your intelligent mind? Is it not being conformed to the world - the world opinion - all in the name of wisdom?

Existence of God

Long time ago, I began talking to a colleague of mine about God. In no time he said, "If there is God show Him to me; I will surely believe." I quickly understood what he meant by it and withdrew from the conversation. How to prove the existence of God? What he was asking me was to employ an empirical method- the method of observation and study. Can God be subjected to such a test? You can put matter to test. It is at your disposal. It can neither conceal nor reveal anything on its own about itself. So you are able to present your findings. But what about knowing a man? Are measurements enough? If he doesn't want to reveal himself to you, is there anything you can do to truly know about him? Do not limitations of empirical method stare into your eye in this regard? How about knowing about God, not to speak of knowing God? If God is transcendental - wholly the other - separate from His creation - where can you begin?

Is there a way to know?

When you are confronted with questions on your existence, perhaps, it is a proof of God's existence. He must have already taken an initiative. If He had taken an initiative it must have been through 'revelation.' 'Revelation' is making known something that is secret or hidden. You look at all the creation. You look at yourself. You know for sure you haven't created you, yourself. The psychologists say that, as children we come to know that we have a head, only when we bump our head against a wall. So even before we come to know that we have a head, we had already been existing! You may admit that you haven't created you, yourself, yet you may venture saying that you don't believe in the existence of God. Is it true that you do not 'believe'? Or are you 'saying' that you do not believe? If we tell ourselves something against what we know, we slowly drift into believing it. It is like telling yourself, 'come on man you don't need to believe that.' You quieten your conscience to seek your own thing.

A few days after my conversation with my colleague about God, one evening, I was returning by my bicycle from college. A student of the class I was teaching was coming towards me. He saw me from a distance. I thought he would respect my presence. As I drew near, I saw him turning his eyes away from me. It aroused the egotistic nature in me. I didn't want to give up. As an old time teacher, I was expecting the students to give utmost regard to me. I slowed down my bicycle, tried to look straight into his eyes and succeeded in drawing his attention. He said, "Good evening sir." I was pleased with it and proceeded. After I went a few steps forwards a thought came to my mind. 'What would he have thought about me?' Surely a sneer! At the outset, did he not see me? Yes, he did. Did he not know that he should respect me? Surely, he did. Perhaps he thought why he should be bothered about my presence. He knew it wouldn't end with just showing respect. I would ask him why he was absent for the class and why his score was so bad and all that. He didn't want to become accountable for all that. He found out an easy way- 'pretend as though he had not seen me'. This incident served as an eye – opener to me. I tried to reason out that my colleague's demand for showing God to him might have something to do with it. Perhaps my colleague's problem with God was just the same. He didn't want to acknowledge God's existence lest he should become accountable to Him. There are certain things God wants him to do and certain other things God doesn't want him to do. Why become accountable to Him, perhaps, was his argument within himself.

"General Revelation" - an answer

I was foolish in forcing my presence upon the student in spite of his unwillingness. Paul, a great theologian of the first century A.D., talks about God's general revelation. It is recorded in the Holy Bible. He says that God has already revealed Himself and that He does not force Himself upon any one. He says, 'since what may be known about God is plain to them, because God has made it plain to them. For since the creation of the world God's invisible qualities—his eternal power and divine nature—have been clearly seen, being understood from what has been made, so that people are without excuse.' (Ro 1:19, 20). When you look at the creation and look at yourself, something is conveyed to you. It is His general revelation in nature. Man is obligated to respond to this. The created should long to relate himself with the creator – the source of his being. According to Paul, when man is able to sense the existence of God in the creation, he is supposed to respond in praise and gratitude. Yes, there is an invisible hand behind me and how wonderfully I am made, should be his response. David, a king says, 'I praise you because I am fearfully and wonderfully made; your works are wonderful, I know that full well.' (Ps 139:14). Man is supposed to be grateful for his life, his parents, the air he breathes, the water he drinks, the community he lives in etc.

Rejection leads to one deceiving oneself

Paul says, 'For although they knew God, they neither glorified him as God nor gave thanks to him, but their thinking became futile and their foolish hearts were darkened.' (Ro 1:21). A man who rejects God's revelation looks for various ways to put forth an argument to deny the existence of God. He becomes ungrateful. A person who rejects God's revelation in nature looks for some way to assert himself. He makes a god for himself. The vacuum he finds in himself he tries to fill with an idol made of his hands. He knows fully well that the God who revealed His qualities to him is totally different from His creation. Equating God with anything which comes to the mind, however lofty the thought might be, is an insult to God. Paul says, 'Although they claimed to be wise, they became fools and exchanged the glory of the immortal God for images made to look like a mortal human being and birds and animals and reptiles.' 'They exchanged the truth about God for a lie, and worshiped and served created things rather than the Creator—who is forever praised. Amen.' (Ro 1:22, 23&25). Paul considers such people self-assertive who deceive themselves.

Paul says that God gives them up. A man, who deliberately chooses to live by himself, loses the fear of God. He tends to lose himself into self-indulgence. How wretched he can become we can't

4

even imagine. Any sensible person will react in shock when he sees a perverted man. Paul minces no words in expressing the truth about these people who reject God's general revelation. He says, 'Therefore God gave them over in the sinful desires of their hearts to sexual impurity for the degrading of their bodies with one another.' 'Because of this, God gave them over to shameful lusts. Even their women exchanged natural sexual relations for unnatural ones. In the same way the men also abandoned natural relations with women and were inflamed with lust for one another. Men committed shameful acts with other men, and received in themselves the due penalty for their error.' (Ro 1:24, 26, 27). Paul's description of the perverted society in his time 2000 years ago fits exactly to the present perverted society we see in this world.

Social reformers are clueless to find a reason for all that is happening in the world. How shocking it is to see human life in its display in our dailies! We may pass by saying that 'the society has always been the same.' Is it not our responsibility to dig deep and find out the root cause for all this? Paul sees in all this the role of the human mind which rejected God's revelation. Paul says, 'Furthermore, just as they did not think it worthwhile to retain the knowledge of God, so God gave them over to a depraved mind, so that they do what ought not to be done. They have become filled with every kind of wickedness, evil, greed and depravity. They are full of envy, murder, strife, deceit and malice. They are gossips, slanderers, God-haters, insolent, arrogant and boastful; they invent ways of doing evil; they disobey their parents; they have no understanding, no fidelity, no love, no mercy. Although they know God's righteous decree that those who do such things deserve death, they not only continue to do these very things but also approve of those who practice them.' (Ro 1:28-32).

Now, can we say that man's problem is with the knowledge of the existence of God? Is not his problem with the rejection of the knowledge? Does he not 'believe' there is God? Or does he want to only 'tell himself' that there is no God? David an Old Testament king says, 'The fool says in his heart, "There is no God." (Ps. 14:1f). How free man is in doing this! Who is he fooling by his freedom? Freedom is a great gift to mankind. Freedom causes openness of mind. The mind is the source of all rationality. Rationality should lead man to become sensible in his decisions.

Acceptance leads to "Special Revelation" - His word

Supposing there are some who see His eternal power and divine nature in creation and choose to obey, where will it lead them? Is there a higher level of revelation? What does God want them to do? Does He have a plan in their individual lives? If He has one how will He communicate it? God has to communicate, primarily, to the people, as people of a generation and also to a person as a responsible person created by God. Further, this communication may have to be in the form of a commandment or a warning or a word of encouragement or a word of prophecy. This prophecy may relate to a particular immediate situation or to a near future situation or even to a far off future situation. When God communicates it, this should invariably be in the language of the group, since happenings in the final analysis relate to a community of a generation in the chain of generations. The communication has to be relevant to the immediate situation in a generation along with a universal statement for all situations and for all generations. For such communication, no wonder, God may have to choose different persons in different ages. Obviously it cannot be a one-time message. These persons when they speak with God's authority, they cause people to listen and to obey His word. Further, when they speak God's word, it must be committed to writing to communicate it to the immediate and also to the future generations. For collection of all these writings, God may have to oversee not only their writings but also their preservation as one book. All this happened in the course of human history with a book called the Bible!

The word Bible is an English word translated from a Greek word 'biblos'. In turn this Greek word is from the Latin word 'biblia', a plural word. So the Bible, the book, is in fact a collection of 66 books - 39 in the Old Testament and 27 in the New Testament. The two categories show God's two main covenants with His people. The latter is connected with human salvation through His Son. These books are written by 40 men over a period of approximately 1500 years. The Bible is linked with human history as God chose to reveal Himself progressively. A substantial part of it is narration. We see a thread of continuity of purpose in the books and in their order of arrangement. It reveals that God has a plan in the community life and in individual lives of men. God places His word - the Bible - in the hands of those who acknowledge His revelation in nature. Their obedience to general revelation leads them to a higher revelation called 'special revelation'. The Bible begins with God and His initiative. 'In the beginning God created the heavens and the earth.' (Ge 1:1). Biblical time is a linear time. It talks of a definite time of beginning and of a definite time of closing of human history. The Bible records, 'Then I saw "a new heaven and a new earth," for the first heaven and the first earth had passed away, and there was no longer any sea.' (Rev 21:1)

The writers were men of varying social and educational levels. Some were statesmen, some were kings, some were philosophers and some were ordinary men from different walks of life. God gave them His word to be presented according to their level of expression in their cultural setting. It is in prose and poetry containing history, science, philosophy sociology, literature and other branches. But the Bible is not there to compete with any one of these branches as it encompasses all these. It proceeds with a theological purpose of offering deliverance to man from sin. It is amazing to note that the Bible, in spite of many attempts on it to annihilate it, has overcome all. It is handed down from cover to cover secure. People see the hand of God – His superintending role – in inspiring the writers and also in collecting and preserving their writings. We see that no author in the Bible projects himself. The reader confronts none else but God, while reading the Bible. In the Bible we see the plan of God being unfolded.

Plan of God

At a University level seminar on 'rights of women', a woman professor made a scathing attack on the Bible. She said that the Bible is the root cause of all the discrimination against women. She questioned the logic behind presenting woman being made out of man. Her argument may sound logical at the surface of it. But we need to give a deep thought to it. If the existence of God is accepted and if creation is seen as His handiwork, is it difficult to accept God as a transcendental deity? The

Bible presents Him as the Maker of heaven and earth, the sea, and everything in them. (Ps. 146:6f). If He is transcendental, the humanity has only its created identity. If we work human generations backwards only a couple remains- a man and a woman. If God had created man and woman separately, there would be two humanities - not one. But the Bible says that God created woman out of man making both of them one humanity. A rational man loves to express his solidarity with this one humanity. Paul, while speaking to the learned men in the meeting of Areopagus in Athens, says, 'from one man he made all the nations, that they should inhabit the whole earth; and he marked out their appointed times in history and the boundaries of their lands. God did this so that they would seek him and perhaps reach out for him and find him, though he is not far from any one of us.' (Ac 17:26, 27). Paul presents God as the Lord of the nations with a plan to reveal His purpose to mankind. He declares Him as the Lord of human history.

Man's alienation from God

The Bible says that God formed Adam out of the dust of the ground and breathed into his nostrils the breath of life and made Eve from the rib of Adam, after causing him to fall into a deep sleep. He placed them in the Garden of Eden. He told them to be fruitful and multiply. He permitted them to eat any fruit from the trees in the garden, except the one from the tree of the knowledge of good and evil. He told them that they would die if they ate it. It is to make them test for themselves their freedom - either to obey God or to disobey. The Bible talks about an enemy of God and man-Satan. He created doubt in their minds on the benevolence of God and told them that their eyes would be opened once they ate the fruit. He lured them by saying that they would be like God and that they could be on their own. They fell into his trap and ate the fruit. The Bible says that sin entered their life and they were driven away from the Garden of Eden by God.

Their backs turned towards God, they move from the Garden of Eden to the wide open world. It is a journey from light towards darkness. The sin of the couple was only disobedience to the word of God. They multiplied and their sin also multiplied. Their elder son Cain tried to please God on his own terms. When he failed, he killed Abel, their younger son who received God's favour. Generations increased on earth. Lamech married two women and boasted of killing a young man in rivalry. There comes a time when God was grieved. 'The LORD saw how great the wickedness of the human race had become on the earth, and that every inclination of the thoughts of the human heart was only evil all the time. The LORD regretted that he had made human beings on the earth, and his heart was deeply troubled.' 'Now the earth was corrupt in God's sight and was full of violence.' (Ge 6:5, 6, 11) 'So the LORD said, "I will wipe from the face of the earth the human race I have created—and with them the animals, the birds and the creatures that move along the ground—for I regret that I have made them." But Noah found favour in the eyes of the LORD.' 'So God said to Noah, "I am going to put an end to all people, for the earth is filled with violence because of them. I am surely going to destroy both them and the earth. So make yourself an ark of cypress wood; make rooms in it and coat it with pitch inside and out.' (Ge 6:7 - 8, 13 and 14)

God delivered Noah, his wife, three sons and three daughters- in-law from the deluge. Generations multiplied again. But man remained the same. They had one language and a common speech. They wanted to defy God and belittle the deluge in the days of Noah. 'They said to each other, "Come, let's make bricks and bake them thoroughly." They used brick instead of stone, and tar for mortar. Then they said, "Come, let us build ourselves a city, with a tower that reaches to the heavens, so that we may make a name for ourselves; otherwise we will be scattered over the face of the whole earth."' (Ge 11:3, 4) It is man against God for his own detriment. So God said, 'Come, let us go down and confuse their language so they will not understand each other." So the LORD scattered them from there over all the earth, and they stopped building the city.' (Ge 11:7, 8) Thus languages arose and nations arose on the face of the earth. Some anthropologists trace the origin of the basic races in the world today to the three sons of Noah.

God calls a man

Generations increased and the Bible records a time when no one knew the one true Living God. God's purposes now boil down to dealing with the world through the offspring of one person. God calls

Abram (an Asian). 'The LORD had said to Abram, "Go from your country, your people and your father's household to the land I will show you. "I will make you into a great nation, and I will bless you; I will make your name great, and you will be a blessing. I will bless those who bless you, and whoever curses you I will curse; and all peoples on earth will be blessed through you."' (Ge 12:1-3). Abram obeys God and sets out on a journey. God reckons his faith as righteousness. God tells him, "'As for me, this is my covenant with you: You will be the father of many nations. No longer will you be called Abram; your name will be Abraham, for I have made you a father of many nations.' (Ge.17:4, 5). The Bible records that through Abraham, Isaac and through Isaac, Jacob and through Jacob the twelve tribes of Israel originate. But how is He going to bless all the families of the earth? What is this blessing after all?

God's tool - a nation?

Through the obedience of one individual God has a plan to execute to deal with the world. 'I will make you very fruitful; I will make nations of you, and kings will come from you.' (Ge 17:6). True to His promise God makes the twelve tribes of Israel a nation after delivering them from the Egyptian bondage in the leadership of Moses. At Mount Sinai, God asks Moses to speak to the Israelites on His behalf. "You yourselves have seen what I did to Egypt, and how I carried you on eagles' wings and brought you to myself. Now if you obey me fully and keep my covenant, then out of all nations you will be my treasured possession. Although the whole earth is mine, you will be for me a kingdom of priests and a holy nation.' These are the words you are to speak to the Israelites."' 'The people all responded together, "We will do everything the LORD has said." So Moses brought their answer back to the LORD.' (Ex 19:4-6, 8) So God forms a nation for Himself and leads them to the land He promised to Abraham in the leadership of Joshua. 'So Joshua took the entire land, just as the LORD had directed Moses, and he gave it as an inheritance to Israel according to their tribal divisions. Then the land had rest from war.' (Jos 11:23).

God intends to rule the nation of Israel directly. But they have different plans. They want Samuel the prophet to speak to God about their plans. 'So all the elders of Israel gathered together and came to Samuel at Ramah. They said to him, "You are old, and your sons do not follow your ways; now appoint a king to lead us, such as all the other nations have." But when they said, "Give us a king to lead us," this displeased Samuel; so he prayed to the LORD. And the LORD told him: "listen to all that the people are saying to you; it is not you they have rejected, but they have rejected me as their king.' 'Now listen to them; but warn them solemnly and let them know what the king who will reign over them will claim as his rights."' (1 Sa. 8:4-7, 9). Samuel anoints Saul as the first king of Israel according to God's choice. Later when Saul disobeys God's word, God rejects him. God chooses David in his place and asks Samuel to anoint David as king. God calls David a man after His own heart and promises that his lineage will rule the kingdom for ever. After David's death, Prophet Nathan anoints Solomon, his son as king. The kingdom flourishes under his rule. Solomon's wisdom becomes known to far off nations. After his death the rebellion divides the kingdom into two - the Northern kingdom Israel and the Southern kingdom Judah. Different families rule the Northern kingdom while David's lineage continues in the Southern kingdom, Judah.

In the Northern kingdom Jeroboam the first king does evil in the eyes of the Lord. After he dies his successors continue in his ways, making the people of Israel do evil in the eyes of the Lord. The Bible records this after the reign of each king: 'He did evil in the eyes of the LORD, following the ways of Jeroboam and committing the same sin Jeroboam had caused Israel to commit.' (1 Ki 15:34). God sends His men time and again to speak His word to the kings to warn them. Elijah is the greatest of these prophets. Finally God uses the Assyrian kingdom as His instrument to put an end to the northern kingdom. The Southern kingdom continues but some of the kings continue in the sin of the Northern kingdom. (2 Ch. 33:9). God sends His prophets time and again to warn them. Jeremiah, the prophet of God, prophesies the fall of Judah. The Babylonian Empire puts an end to the kingdom of Judah and takes the people captive to Babylon. It marks the end of a great nation. When it was no longer a nation how could this be a blessing to all the nations of the earth?

God's choice - a king?

As Jeremiah prophesied, the Jews return to their homeland after seventy years of captivity. They begin to search the Scriptures to find fulfilment to their expectation of a king and a kingdom. They find that the Scriptures point to the Davidic king their redeemer- the one promised by God. '"…I will set him over my house and my kingdom forever; his throne will be established forever."' (1 Ch. 17:14). They remember the interpretation of Nebuchadnezzar's dream by Daniel while in the Babylonian captivity. According to Daniel after the fall of the Babylonian kingdom, three more kingdoms rule and during the rule of the third kingdom, God establishes His kingdom. (Da 2:36-40, 44). Years roll by and the expectation is handed down the generations. Just as Daniel interpreted the dream we see kingdoms rising and falling. The Babylonian kingdom falls. The Medo-Persian kingdom and later the Greek kingdom fall in that line. The fourth, the Roman kingdom rules the then known world. Then all eyes look for the kingdom which God establishes. Who is this king, the redeemer, the Messiah who is to take over during the rule of the Romans? No such sign is seen by the people who are looking expectantly for the Davidic king. During 400 years before the intervention of God, the prophets remain silent and the priesthood remains silent. The princes and people also remain silent. In their silence God's plan continues to operate.

Intervention of God

If God is the Lord of History, is it not His prerogative to intervene in human history, in His own way? Jewish expectations of a Davidic king have to be in line with His personal plans. In the book of Ezekiel God makes known His plans through the prophet Ezekiel. His concerns are theological. He finds fault with the shepherds of Israel- God's appointed caretakers over the people of Israel. After listing the various areas in which the shepherds violated God's concerns, He promises His people His personal intervention. 'This is what the Sovereign LORD says: I am against the shepherds and will hold them accountable for my flock. I will remove them from tending the flock so that the shepherds can no longer feed themselves. I will rescue my flock from their mouths, and it will no longer be food for them. "'For this is what the Sovereign LORD says: I myself will search for my sheep and look after them.' (Eze. 34:10, 11) He tells His people, "'...You are my sheep, the sheep of my pasture, and I am your God, declares the Sovereign LORD.'"" (Eze. 34:31). These prophecies intrigue the Jews and make them search the Scriptures all the more for a better understanding of a promised king. Does God want to rule directly again? What can be the nature of such a rule? Any way it appears that God Himself wants to come on to the stage!

God's choice – God-Man!

The ruler of the earlier kingdom- Alexander, the Greek emperor makes sure that all people in his kingdom speak common Greek to become familiar with Greek culture. Communication in Greek brings people across the nations as one people. After the Greek kingdom the Roman kingdom lays grand high ways all over the world to connect with Rome. Easy transport makes people travel conveniently and it creates a common platform. The Romans make sure people live in peace in their kingdom suppressing all rebellions. During this fourth kingdom, according to the prophecy of Daniel, a new kingdom is taking shape. Perhaps, Paul has in mind the world developments when he says, 'But when the set time had fully come, God sent his Son, born of a woman, born under the law' (Gal 4:4). Who is this Son of God? Is He also called as the Son of David? What does Paul say about this person? Why do the Jews confine the role of the coming king only for themselves? Have they forgotten the second part of God's promise to Abraham? Don't they realise that the Messiah is for the blessing of all? By the time Paul wrote his letters, the Jews had become so obsessed with themselves that they called all others uncircumcised, separate from Christ - the Messiah, excluded from citizenship in Israel, foreigners to the covenants of the promise and without hope and without God in the world.

What is God's promise to Abraham concerning the rest of the mankind? "'...and through your offspring all nations on earth will be blessed, because you have obeyed me.'" (Ge 22:18). God's promise is to the Jews and to the rest of the nations as well. The word 'offspring' means seed. Who is this seed? Paul links God's Son to the promised seed of Abraham. He says, 'The promises were spoken to Abraham and to his seed. The Scripture does not say "and to seeds," meaning many people, but "and to your seed," meaning one person, who is Christ' (Gal 3:16). How mysterious are God's ways!

God-Man - Jesus Christ

While writing a letter to the Romans, Paul presents Jesus Christ as God-Man, the promised seed of Abraham, the promised king in the lineage of David. 'Paul, a servant of Christ Jesus, called to be an apostle and set apart for the gospel of God — the gospel he promised beforehand through his prophets in the Holy Scriptures regarding his Son, who as to his earthly life was a descendant of David, and who through the Spirit of holiness was appointed the Son of God in power by his resurrection from the dead: Jesus Christ our Lord.' (Ro 1:1-4) It is God Himself coming into human history. John solves the mystery of the plural used in the creation story of the Bible. In this God said, 'Let us make man in our image, in our likeness.' According to John, the Son of God is the eternal Son, 'The Word of God.' John says, 'In the beginning was the Word, and the Word was with God, and the Word was God. He was with God in the beginning. Through him all things were made; without him nothing was made that has been made.' (Jn. 1:1-3).

Jesus – "the Final Revelation"

Seven hundred years before the birth of Jesus Christ, Isaiah prophesied: 'therefore the Lord himself will give you a sign: The virgin will conceive and give birth to a son, and will call him Immanuel.' (Isa 7:14); 'For to us a child is born, to us a son is given, and the government will be on his shoulders. And he will be called Wonderful Counsellor, Mighty God, Everlasting Father, Prince of Peace.' (Isa 9:6). Luke records the fulfilment of the prophecies 700 years later: 'In the sixth month of Elizabeth's pregnancy, God sent the angel Gabriel to Nazareth, a town in Galilee, to a virgin pledged to be married to a man named Joseph, a descendant of David. The virgin's name was Mary. The angel went to her and said, "Greetings, you who are highly favoured! The Lord is with you." Mary was greatly troubled at his words and wondered what kind of greeting this might be. But the angel said to her, "Do not be afraid, Mary; you have found favour with God. You will conceive and give birth to a son, and you are to call him Jesus. He will be great and will be called the Son of the Most High. The Lord God will give him the throne of his father David, and he will reign over Jacob's descendants forever; his kingdom will never end." "How will this be," Mary asked the angel, "since I am a virgin?" The angel answered, "The Holy Spirit will come on you, and the power of the Most High will overshadow you. So the holy one to be born will be called the Son of God. Even Elizabeth your relative is going to have a child in her old age, and she who was said to be unable to conceive is in her sixth month. For no word from God will ever fail." "I am the Lord's servant," Mary answered. "May your word to me be fulfilled." Then the angel left her.' (Lk. 1:26-38).

Matthew also records from Joseph's point of view: 'this is how the birth of Jesus the Messiah came about: His mother Mary was pledged to be married to Joseph, but before they came together, she was found to be pregnant through the Holy Spirit. Because Joseph her husband was faithful to the law, and yet did not want to expose her to public disgrace, he had in mind to divorce her quietly. But after he had considered this, an angel of the Lord appeared to him in a dream and said, "Joseph son of David, do not be afraid to take Mary home as your wife, because what is conceived in her is from the Holy Spirit. She will give birth to a son, and you are to give him the name Jesus, because he will save his people from their sins." All this took place to fulfil what the Lord had said through the prophet: "The virgin will conceive and give birth to a son, and they will call him Immanuel" (which means "God with us"). When Joseph woke up, he did what the angel of the Lord had commanded him and took Mary home as his wife.' (Mt 1:18-24).

Luke records that Joseph is from the lineage of David: 'So Joseph also went up from the town of Nazareth in Galilee to Judea, to Bethlehem the town of David, because he belonged to the house and line of David. He went there to register with Mary, who was pledged to be married to him and was expecting a child. While they were there, the time came for the baby to be born, and she gave birth to her firstborn, a son. She wrapped him in cloths and placed him in a manger, because there was no guest room available for them.' (Lk. 2:4-7). Jesus is born. Wise men from the East see in Jesus 'the king of the Jews'. 'After Jesus was born in Bethlehem in Judea, during the time of King Herod, Magi from the east came to Jerusalem and asked, "Where is the one who has been born king of the Jews? We saw his star when it rose and have come to worship him."' (Mt. 2:1, 2). They worship Jesus: 'On coming to the house, they saw the child with his mother Mary, and they bowed down and worshiped him. Then they opened their treasures and presented him with gifts of gold, frankincense and myrrh.' (Mt 2:11). The shepherds see in Jesus 'the saviour'. The Angel tells them: 'Today in the town of David a Saviour has been born to you; he is the Messiah, the Lord.' (Lk. 2:11). He is the final revelation of God to man. John says, 'No one has ever seen God, but the one and only Son, who is himself God and is in closest relationship with the Father, has made him known.' (Jn. 1:18).

Contrary to the expectations of the Jews in His time, Jesus was born in a poor carpenter's family. Luke records his childhood days: 'And Jesus grew in wisdom and stature, and in favour with God and man.' (Lk. 2:52). We see in it all that is needed for a balanced growth of a child, in the life of boy Jesus. We see physical, intellectual, spiritual and social areas in a human being. A child needs to grow in all these areas to live a balanced life. All these faculties came under display in the adulthood of Jesus. From the records of the Bible we can infer that Jesus too worked as a carpenter after the death of Joseph, till he was 30 years old. (Mk. 6:3). Jesus took baptism at the age of 30. John, the one who baptized Him, saw these: the heavens opening and the Holy Spirit descending on him in the form of a dove and he heard God speaking from above saying that Jesus is His Son and that He is well pleased with Him. After His baptism the Holy Spirit drove Jesus into the desert to be tempted by the enemy of God - Satan. After 40 days of fasting and prayer, Jesus was tempted by Satan to displease God. But Jesus overcame the temptation. Paul identifies two fountain heads in humanity – one, Adam and the other, Jesus Christ. Adam disregards God's word and remains the fountain head of disobedience and Jesus upholds God's word and becomes the fountain head of obedience. Jesus returned from the desert saying that the kingdom of God is near. He commanded the people to repent and believe in the Gospel. He appointed twelve ordinary men as His disciples.

God's involvement – the public life of Jesus

There is suffering in human life. When we look at the suffering of people these questions come to our mind: What will God do when He looks at human life? Which areas of human life is He interested in? Does God really care for human suffering? Is His intervention an answer to all those who cry out in suffering, 'where is God?' When Jesus began His earthly ministry there was hardly any expectation. People considered Him just as an ordinary carpenter from Galilee.

Sickness

Sickness causes terrible suffering. Some people are born blind and are born deaf and dumb. Epilepsy draws pity from the onlookers. No one likes to look pitiable. Paralysis keeps a man immobile and makes him become dependent on others for most personal needs, which man hates the most. Leprosy is a disease which is looked upon as sin. People keep lepers away from the place of their dwelling. Further, there is the problem of evil spirits possessing people. People possessed by the spirits hurt not only others but also themselves. It looks beyond the onlookers understanding. Those who take care of them always reach the breaking point of helplessness and frustration. Does God have concern for these people? How does the world know that He has concern? Jesus after entering into His earthly ministry immediately responds to these needs of people. Luke records, 'At sunset, the people brought to Jesus all who had various kinds of sickness, and laying his hands on each one, he healed them.' (Lk. 4:40).

Poverty and Hunger

Poverty and hunger go together. The reasons for poverty in the world can be obtained from a real life situation during the days of Nehemiah. If the size of the family is large, it causes shortage of food. During the days of famine the worst hit are the poor. They mortgage the small property they have. Once their earnings do not match with their expenses and loan interest, they fall into further debt- miry clay. The taxes they have to pay become a burden all the more. The rich hoard the grain for profit and oppress the poor for their prosperity.

(Ne 5:1-4) How does God take care of the poor? What is His warning to the rich?

Jesus always has a comforting word to the poor. 'Looking at his disciples, he said: "Blessed are you who are poor, for yours is the kingdom of God. Blessed are you who hunger now, for you will be satisfied. Blessed are you who weep now, for you will laugh.' (Lk. 6:20, 21). He says that His father takes care of the sparrows, and so He will surely take care of their needs. He says, 'For the pagans run after all these things, and your heavenly Father knows that you need them. But seek first his kingdom and his righteousness, and all these things will be given to you as well.' (Mt 6:32, 33). Jesus has always a severe word for the rich. 'Then Jesus said to his disciples, "Truly I tell you, it is hard for someone who is rich to enter the kingdom of heaven. Again I tell you, it is easier for a camel to go through the eye of a needle than for someone who is rich to enter the kingdom of God."' (Mt 19:23, 24). His concern for the hungry is evident. He says, '"I have compassion for these people; they have already been with me three days and have nothing to eat. If I send them home hungry, they will collapse on the way, because some of them have come a long distance."' (Mk. 8:2,3). He miraculously feeds thousands of them at two different times.

Widening gap – the rich and the poor

The ever widening gap between the rich and the poor is a matter of great concern to some social reformers. Communism is at work to combat this. Is God concerned about this? How does God look at this? Is He concerned only about the heavenly life of His people? In the days of Moses, the deliverer of Israelites, God rained down manna from heaven to feed them. For forty years He demonstrated His concern for equality. They were to gather each day enough for each one, only for that day - provision for one day at a time. Though some gathered more and some less, when they went home and measured, it came up only according to their need. This is social justice at its best. Only God demonstrated it in a community. Accordingly Jesus asks people to pray for their daily bread. This prayer for food is for the coming 24 hours - one day at a time. Jesus asks them not to worry about the next day, 'Therefore do not worry about tomorrow, for tomorrow will worry about itself. Each day has enough trouble of its own.' (Mt 6:34). Some of the rich responded positively. They understood the uncertainty of wealth. Levi, Zacchaeus and later Barnabas are clear willing cases to identify with the poor, dispensing with their wealth. Jesus was thoroughly concerned about the ever widening gap between the rich and the poor. He promoted a life style which amazes those who fight for social justice. There are some who live the life style which Jesus preaches. They live one day at a time with a secure feeling- their trust in God's provision.

Gender disparity

Gender disparity! How ridiculous it is to treat the female population differently! Are not men and women equal in God's sight? The Bible records,'...God created man in his own image, in the image of God He created him; male and female he created them.' (Ge 1:27). Here 'man' refers to humanity and it consists of male and female. It is evident that their status is equal but their functions are different. Male and female complement each other. Each one makes the other full. As the humanity is to be one, God made Eve from Adam. We cannot infer from it that Adam is superior to Eve. In his fallen nature man began behaving as though he was superior to woman. This resulted in male chauvinism in the society. Israelites, God's chosen people, the Jews, were no exception. Women were deprived of their due functioning in the Jewish society. Men began looking down upon women boasting about their birth as men. When God intervenes in human history does He show his concern about the state of affairs in the society in this regard?

Jesus, as a Jewish young man, relates himself with women as He relates himself with men. He chooses to converse with a Samaritan woman breaking the walls of separation between Jews and Samaritans on one hand and man and woman on the other. John records, 'When a Samaritan woman came to draw water, Jesus said to her, "Will you give me a drink?" (His disciples had gone into the town to buy food.) The Samaritan woman said to him, "You are a Jew and I am a Samaritan woman. How can you ask me for a drink?" (For Jews do not associate with Samaritans.)' (Jn 4:7-9). The records tell us that she was infamous in that village. But Jesus gave her dignity to hold her head high to address people. Women find an easy access to Jesus. Once Jesus tells a woman, "Woman, you have great faith! Your request is granted." (Mt 15:28) She feels honoured. He honours a poor widow at the temple treasury. "'Truly I tell you,' he said, 'this poor widow has put in more than all the others. All these people gave their gifts out of their wealth; but she out of her poverty put in all she had to live on.'" (Lk. 21:3, 4) He happily allows a sinful woman's emotional anointing of His feet. He doesn't show embarrassment. Instead He makes her feel honourable. (Lk 7:44) Jesus respects woman as a person and safeguards the dignity God bestowed on women.

Marginalising some people

In the society we find some people giving themselves up to deceitful means of earning money. Some people work for others violating the interests of their own people for their living. Some become addicts to drunkenness and other habits. Some women sell themselves away for some reason or another. The society keeps them marginalised and looks down upon them. Is there no hope for such people? Is it just to treat them as untouchables? Can't they have access to human dignity? If God were to intervene in human affairs what would be His attitude towards such people?

Jesus, unlike the teachers and spiritual leaders of His time goes close to the marginalised people. He becomes accessible to people who are set aside by the Jewish community. He enjoys time with them eating and drinking. The leaders find it difficult to place Him in their spiritual order. When He takes Levi, a tax collector as His disciple, Levi throws a grand dinner inviting many including his colleagues. They sit around Jesus and enjoy themselves in his company eating together. (Mk 2:15-17). The marginalised people slowly get interested in His teaching. 'Now the tax collectors and sinners were all gathering around to hear Jesus. But the Pharisees and the teachers of the law muttered, "This man welcomes sinners and eats with them."' (Lk. 15:1,2). 'On hearing this, Jesus said, "It is not the healthy who need a doctor, but the sick. But go and learn what this means: 'I desire mercy, not sacrifice.' For I have not come to call the righteous, but sinners."' (Mt 9:12, 13) Jesus finds fault with the attitude of people who believe that man does favour to God. Jesus relates well with the Samaritans who were looked down upon by the Jews because of a racial difference. In the story of the good Samaritan Jesus contrasted the merciful attitude of the Samaritan with the uncaring attitude of the Priest and the Levite towards the neighbour. Jesus has a kind word to a woman caught in adultery. When they ask Him to tell them whether they could stone her according to the Law of Moses or leave her, He tells them that the one who is without sin should stone her first. All of them leave. John records, 'Jesus straightened up and asked her, "Woman, where are they? Has no one condemned you?" "No one, sir," she said. "Then neither do I condemn you," Jesus declared. "Go now and leave your life of sin."' (Jn. 8:10, 11). What dignity and honour we see in a forgiven feeling and changed attitude! Jesus acknowledges this attitude seen in people. He says, 'I tell you the truth, the tax collectors and the prostitutes are entering the kingdom of God ahead of you'!

Indifference towards children!

Children are children. They are gullible. They are vulnerable to abuse. Time and again we read in the Newspapers of serious crimes committed against them. Even when they are taken care of no proper importance is given to their individuality. Children are considered objects – of course, objects of love. Parents consider them beings at the receiving end. They are not consulted. Parents think that there is nothing they can contribute to the family. People see hardly anything in them which they can learn from them. The world is indifferent to them. They are considered unimportant in spiritual matters and a nuisance in get-togethers. They are usually kept aside. How does God view at them? Does He not see them as individuals with a will to exercise? Can they relate with Him if they want to?

Jesus considers them as much important as others, as they too are created in the image and likeness of God. He was indignant when they were treated badly. Mark records, 'People were bringing little children to Jesus for him to place his hands on them, but the disciples rebuked them. When Jesus saw this, he was indignant. He said to them, "Let the little children come to me, and do not hinder them, for the kingdom of God belongs to such as these. Truly I tell you, anyone who will not receive the kingdom of God like a little child will never enter it." And he took the children in his arms, placed his hands on them and blessed them.' (Mk 10:13-16). He responded immediately when they were in need. He raised from the dead the young son of a widow and a girl child of an officer.

Bereavement

Millions die each day. How terrible death is! People shudder at the very thought of it. The bereaved mourn for their loved ones. In no time some become poor widows and some, destitute children. Some people lose their own in their old age. They are left alone helpless. The bereaved find no meaning in their existence any longer on earth. How does God view the pain of the bereaved? Does He take death just as a natural phenomenon and ignore it? When God lives among human beings how does He respond to this predicament of man?

Luke records an event where Jesus confronts death: 'Soon afterward, Jesus went to a town called Nain, and his disciples and a large crowd went along with him. As he approached the town gate, a dead person was being carried out—the only son of his mother, and she was a widow. And a large crowd from the town was with her. When the Lord saw her, his heart went out to her and he said, "Don't cry." Then he went up and touched the bier they were carrying him on, and the bearers stood still. He said, "Young man, I say to you, get up!" The dead man sat up and began to talk, and Jesus gave him back to his mother.' (Lk. 7:11-15) On another occasion He heeds to the pleadings of the father of a little girl who is dead. Mark records, 'He took her by the hand and said to her, "Talitha koum!" (Which means "Little girl, I say to you, get up!"). Immediately the girl stood up and began to walk around (she was twelve years old). At this they were completely astonished.' (Mk 5:41, 42). We see His humanness in display when one of His friends, Lazarus, dies. John records, 'When Jesus saw her weeping, and the Jews who had come along with her also weeping, he was deeply moved in spirit and troubled. "Where have you laid him?" he asked. "Come and see, Lord," they replied. Jesus wept." (Jn. 11:33-35). He looks straight into the eye of death. John records, 'When he had said this, Jesus called in a loud voice, "Lazarus, come out!" The dead man came out, his hands and feet wrapped with strips of linen, and a cloth around his face. Jesus said to them, "Take off the grave clothes and let him go.'" (Jn. 11:43, 44). Jesus demonstrates His power over death. The humanity longs for overcoming death. Jesus promises a life which overcomes death.

Communication breakdown

There is conflict in the world because of breakdown in interpersonal relationships. This affects the family first. It spreads to the society and affects the fabric of human life. The reason for breakdown in interpersonal relationships is the attitude of people towards others. Prejudice, egotism, haughty nature, double standards and hypocrisy are some of the elements which negatively influence their attitude. Society is full of people of all kinds. How wonderful it would be if an ideal pattern is presented in interpersonal relationships! How would God relate Himself with people if He were to pitch His tent among them?

John says that God pitched His tent among people. It is Jesus, the Word of God. John says, 'The Word became flesh and made his dwelling among us. We have seen his glory, the glory of the one and only Son, who came from the Father, full of grace and truth.' (Jn. 1:14). It is human tendency to become prejudiced in favour of some and against some others. Jesus hates people displaying double standards and speaking according to their whims and fancies. Jesus points out the double standards, 'For John the Baptist came neither eating bread nor drinking wine and you say, 'He has a demon.' The Son of Man came eating and drinking, and you say, 'Here is a glutton and a drunkard, a friend of tax collectors and sinners." (Lk 7:33, 34). The social life of Jesus Christ is remarkable. He lives amiably among chosen few and also among the crowd. He relates Himself with a family, a couple, two people and a single person the same way He relates Himself with His disciples. He remains the same person when He meets all these people - a person full of grace and truth. He doesn't impose truth or law at the cost of love nor does He show love at the cost of truth or law. When someone does something good, He is ready to commend such a deed and when someone does something wrong, He takes no time to condemn such an act. We never see Him prejudiced against any one. He goes all out to love those who do not deserve love.

His interpersonal relationships are in stark contrast to any person's relationships in society. He shows true humanity. When an officer shows faith in His word, He exclaims before all others the greatness of such faith. This is commendation a person deserves. When Peter, His disciple, comes in His way against the will of God, He calls him Satan. When the Pharisees and Scribes behave hypocritically, He condemns their acts with utter severity. This is a rebuke which the guilty incur. In all these He finds a reason to demonstrate His grace and truth. He was never found to be prejudiced against anyone but on the other hand He showered love on the undeserving. In spite of all the weaknesses a man has, he can receive the love of Jesus. It is beyond all human understanding. It has no reason. It is only because of His grace.

False teaching

Love for teaching is universal. We teach others while failing to teach ourselves the same thing. In the name of wisdom any teaching is promoted. Here, there is the danger of being exposed to false teaching. It spreads like cancer. It eats away the fabric of the society. False teaching on God is all the more dangerous. You become what you believe. In the world we see great teachers and acclaim them as virtuous people. Great philosophers try to explain the mysteries behind human life. Often these go beyond the heads of common men. They may finally give up in frustration saying knowledge of God is granted only to a few blessed people. If God intervenes, how will He make His wisdom available?

Paul says, 'Oh, the depth of the riches of the wisdom and knowledge of God! How unsearchable his judgments, and his paths beyond tracing out! "Who has known the mind of the Lord? Or who has been his counsellor?" "Who has ever given to God, that God should repay them?" For from him and through him and for him are all things. To him be the glory forever! Amen.' (Ro 11:33-36) John records about the teaching of Jesus, 'Not until halfway through the festival did Jesus go up to the temple courts and begin to teach. The Jews there were amazed and asked, "How did this man get such learning without having been taught?"' (Jn. 7:14, 15); '"No one ever spoke the way this man does," the guards replied.' (Jn. 7:46) His teaching was in stark contrast to the teaching of the Pharisees and Scribes. Mathew says, 'When Jesus had finished saying these things, the crowds were amazed at his teaching, because he taught as one who had authority, and not as their teachers of the law.' (Mt 7: 28, 29) Teachers of the law think that it is scholarly to leave matters with loose ends. The philosophers of the world see greatness in leaving everything abstract. Teaching of Jesus always reached the masses unlike the teachers of His time. Mark says, 'With many similar parables Jesus spoke the word to them, as much as they could understand. He did not say anything to them without using a parable. But when he was alone with his own disciples, he explained everything.' (Mk 4:33, 34) The common people in large numbers always listened to him with delight.

Spiritual forces of evil

The fear of the unknown causes havoc in human life. Sorcery and witchcraft are on the increase. These culminate in human sacrifice. The practice of spiritualism is holding families in the grip of fear. The natural by - product of all these practices is superstition which causes enormous damage to daily social life of people. It leads to suspicion on one another. It arrests economic progress and leads the poor into utter poverty. Existence of evil forces is acknowledged for long. These forces have no favouritism. They destroy those who are against them and also those who favour them. Addiction, drunkenness, breakdown of marriages, suicides etc. and fights among countries and races are common everywhere in the world. All these are caused by the evil spirits. They are after human blood - the life. If God were to live among people how would He confront the evil spirits?

Jesus says that no evil spirit fights against another evil spirit to favour man. He says that no kingdom divided against itself will flourish and that a house divided against itself will fall. He says that His kingdom alone favours man. The Bible records of the upsurge of the evil forces during the earthly life of Jesus. He casts out demons and delivers people possessed by the evil spirits. 'So he travelled throughout Galilee, preaching in their synagogues and driving out demons.' (Mk 1:39). The evil spirits confess in public that Jesus is the Son of God. 'In the synagogue there was a man possessed by a demon, an impure spirit. He cried out at the top of his voice, "Go away! What do you want with us, Jesus of Nazareth? Have you come to destroy us? I know who you are—the Holy One of God!'" (Lk. 4:33, 34) Jesus promised the people a life free from the evil forces. Superstition cannot find a place in such life. As stated above these evil spirits are still at work today and the battle in the heavenly realms, as Paul puts it, continues. Jesus is still dealing with these evil forces. His people can defeat these forces through the power of the Holy Spirit today.

A problem common to everyone - sin

A man may not be as bad as his fellow man is. But he has the tendency and potentiality to be fully bad. In spite of all the evil appearing in the world, we clearly see that man is still a moral being. He is concerned about good and bad in human character. He frames rules for morality and wants to live by them. 'Conscience' a person's keeper, the sense of what is right and what is wrong, is the key agent which causes concern in him for morality. So far as his desire is concerned things appear to be all right. It is in keeping morals in his everyday life he finds himself wanting. It is so very conspicuous that human conduct, the ethical behaviour, is not up to the standards of general morality. There appears a conflict between the standard set in his mind and his ability to live according to the standard. As a result of continuous conflict he settles down to a notion that calls the gap a lapse, an error, a failure or at the most a mistake. However lightly we may treat the gap, its consequence in human life looks disastrous. The so called religious people are no exception. Paul says, 'There will be terrible times in the last days. People will be lovers of themselves, lovers of money, boastful, proud, abusive, disobedient to their parents, ungrateful, unholy, without love, unforgiving, slanderous, without self-control, brutal, not lovers of the good, treacherous, rash, conceited, lovers of pleasure rather than lovers of God — having a form of godliness but denying its power. Have nothing to do with such people.' (2 Ti 3:1-5) The Bible calls a spade a spade. So it calls the gap 'Sin'.

Deliverance from the problem of sin - God's method

Supposing God were to live here in our midst how would He react to this? If He feels so bad how would He act to change the sad state of affairs? If He limits Himself to time and space which method would He employ to enable all human beings to make up the gap? Then, what of the coming generations? Does He repeat His visits?

Jesus of Nazareth never appears hasty in correcting people. We do not see Him playing the role of a social reformer trying to set people in order - from the rulers down to the common man. On the other hand we see Him moving with them in warm relationship. He employs the Biblical word 'sin' to describe the nature and activity of a person. But in His teaching through parables, He emphasises a concept called change of heart. He claims Himself to be from above and puts before them their obligation to trust Him. Perhaps in recognition of the desire for forgiveness in a paralytic, on one occasion, He tells him that his sins are forgiven. When the religious people felt offended, He tells them that they should know that He has authority in this world to forgive sins. This baffles them. How nice it would have been if it had ended there. In a short time from then, Jesus begins, speaking about laying His life as a ransom for many. He told them that he would be handed over to the Romans by His own, to be killed. He added saying that He was going according to the prophecies but the one who hands Him over would not find an excuse. This speaks of human responsibility in spite of God's sovereignty. He told them also that He would rise again from the dead on the third day. Whether the disciples saw any relationship between human sin and the blood of Jesus, we do not know. But very soon, on the eve of their festival of redemption, the Passover, He offered them bread and wine telling them that they symbolize His broken body and shed blood for the forgiveness of their sins. True to what He had told them, the following day He was crucified. The third day He rose from the dead leaving the grave empty. His followers in large numbers testify to the fact that He died and rose again on the third day.

Implications of the death and resurrection of Jesus

If Jesus were what He said He was, should it not be our own natural response to trust Him? Cannot God, have the prerogative to decide how He should deal with human sin and how He should accept us into His kingdom? We can observe the events leading to the death and resurrection of Jesus Christ. The Bible doesn't permit us to observe and leave those at that. It makes the interpretation and application obligatory. We respond to the facts observed by saying, 'what does it mean to me? And how am I to take it?' Paul, a Jewish theologian and a scholar, who was fervently persecuting the followers of Jesus after His death, was confronted by the resurrected Jesus; he repents and accepts Jesus as the Lord. God reveals to Paul the implications of the event of the death and resurrection of Jesus Christ in human life. (I Co. 15:3,4) It is only through the blood of Jesus Christ on the Cross all others in the world are made one with the Jews. (Eph. 2:13; 3:6) That is why Paul makes it the central event for putting faith and receiving the forgiveness of sins in individual lives both for the Jews and the others in the world.

Paul argues at length to prove that non-Jews commit sins and incur the wrath of God. Then turns to the Jews and proves that they commit the same sins in spite of the Law they have in their hands. He makes a universal statement saying that there is no one righteous and that all have sinned and fallen short of His glory. (Ro 3:9, 23) The word picture he presents makes us see that we long for God's glory in store for us and attempt to reach it but always fall short of it. How true the picture fits the present situation where people try with all religious fervour to earn God's favour! If God is perfect, He expects 100 per cent perfection in man to reach Him. We can't expect to earn 100 per cent even if we grow into perfection progressively along with our age. Principles of morality of non-Jews and the Law of the Jews are of no avail. Paul interprets that God sets aside the system of grading of morality and brings out the Good News.

Good News – the Gospel – 'the all' at your yes

This is a clear case for shouting aloud. At a time when man is in desperate need of a saviour to redeem him from the punishment for sin, God reveals His plan of salvation. He offers salvation to men, which can be received freely through faith in the death and resurrection of His Son. He commits this Good News to men, the disciples of Jesus Christ, to announce it to the whole world. There is a good reason for enthusiasm in those who have understood God's plan of salvation and who have received the Good News. Paul calls this 'Good News' 'justification by faith.' Paul employs a legal term 'justification', which a judge uses to declare an accused not guilty. God, the judge says, 'you are acquitted - you are set free'. He says that the basis for His grace is the blood of His son Jesus Christ. According to Paul, this is the Good News – the Gospel. (Ro 3:26). He says that there is a condition for receiving this acquittal. The condition is faith. It is only a means. It is faith in the completed work of God. (Gal 2:16). This faith-your 'yes'-begins with conviction in the mind and leads to commitment of the will and reception in the heart.

God's demand of righteousness - side-lined?

Jesus said that He had not come to abolish the Law but had come to fulfil it. He said that the Law will last till the smallest letter and the least stroke of a pen are fulfilled. It is true that He fulfilled the Law. But how about His followers, about whom Paul says they are justified. Does Paul say that there is no need to fulfil the Law? Paul tells the Ephesian believers that they are saved by grace through faith. He says that they are saved without a bit of their effort to do good works. But he calls them the workmanship of God in Christ to do the good works God laid before them. What is it to be God's workmanship? Is it possible for them to be good and to do good? Paul sees the possibility in the death and resurrection of Jesus Christ. Why did God give up Jesus, His Son to be crucified on the cross and why did He raise Him again from the dead? Had He left Him among the dead we would have acclaimed the sacrifice of His Son. His followers would have gained a point before the world. But God willed it otherwise. Besides being the first fruits from the dead which leaves hope for His followers to overcome death and live with Him eternally, Jesus, now, through His Spirit, is the power in His follower's lives. He lives in them. The Spirit of Christ now enables the followers to fulfil 'the Law', which is resurrected as 'the Christian ethic', the good works, not to earn merit but to display God's love towards men. They now hope to show forth the righteousness which was not possible earlier.

What is righteousness after all? It is Christ-likeness. God's purpose in electing people for Himself is to see Christ-likeness being formed in them. For this, God sent the Spirit of His Son into the hearts of the followers. They can, now, call God their daddy. (Gal 4:6). They receive

God's approval when He judges the world as they showed obedience in receiving the Good News and marched forward step by step into His Son's likeness.

Paul does not shirk away from talking about the benefits children of God receive here on earth. He is very much conscious about the multi sided meaning, the word 'salvation' possesses. He sees safety, health and prosperity along with deliverance from sin in God's promise of salvation to mankind. But to him deliverance from sin is the key factor in salvation. While talking to children of God about love of God at length, he questions, 'He who did not spare his own Son, but gave him up for us all—how will he not also, along with him, graciously give us all things?' (Ro 8:32).

Along with 'justification' which brings the court room picture into our mind, the Bible employs many other word pictures to convey the meaning of God's salvation. The word 'atonement' brings to our mind the priestly work in a temple. Atonement is reconciliation between God and man as a result of his sins being covered up. The word 'redemption' is a word which was used in a market place. The slaves obtain their freedom when a ransom is paid. It conveys the meaning of Jesus buying people with a price which is His precious blood. A person who accepts the Good News receives salvation in all its splendour.

'Yes or No' in its crucial climax

Anyone embracing materialism confronts a direct question from Jesus. He says, "What does it profit a man if he gains the whole world and loses his own soul?" What does it mean? Is not the world 'all that' is? No. Jesus speaks of a life which baffles the materialist. He says, "I have come to give life and life in all its abundance." What life is he talking about to men who are very much alive? He calls this life neither exclusively physical nor exclusively spiritual but a life which combines both. He calls it eternal life. It is 'the all' – the earthly and heavenly. This is made available for anyone who believes in the Gospel.

'Yes' or 'No' is our response in all walks of life when we face situations of choice. We enjoy the benefits or bear the consequences of our choice. When a wrong choice is made that relates to temporal life, however severe the consequences may be they end with this life we live.

'Yes or No' reaches its climactic end when it relates to Good News, God offers. The consequences naturally are eternal. The choice takes us to our destiny. Man's ego finds no meaning, if all it has to do is with this short span of life. It finds its meaning only when there is eternity.

Every gift needs a recipient and every offer needs acceptance. John says that God gave us Jesus as a gift because of His great love for us. (Jn. 3:16). He says that this offer is applicable to both the non-Jews and the Jews. Whether a non-Jew or a Jew, He says, becomes a child of God, when he receives Jesus and puts his trust in Him. (Jn. 1:10-13). What a great privilege it is to become a child of God! Jesus is His only Son. But He adopts those who believe in the Gospel as His children. Now, Jesus becomes the first born and those who believe in Him are his younger brothers and sisters. The public life of Jesus in those days can now be repeated on this earth. The men and women who are now fulfilling that role of Jesus are none other but the believers in Jesus Christ who are spread around the globe, cutting across all barriers of language, race, caste, creed and culture.

When the Gospel is presented, men face a choice – 'Yes' or 'No'. Freedom of man, which God honours, comes to its crucial test with the choice presented in the Gospel. The destiny of man finally stares in his eye. You have come of age. That is why you have understood the Gospel and its implications. You have a choice before you which you never faced before. You can say 'Yes' if you want to. Your 'Yes' finally offers 'the all' to you. If you are willing, you may please pray like this.

"Creator God, I believe in your existence. I believe that you sent your Son Jesus Christ into this world for me. I believe that He died for me. I believe that there is forgiveness of sins through the blood of your son. Please forgive my sins and receive me into your family. Please send the Spirit of your resurrected Son into my heart and enable me to turn away from all evil ways and walk in the path of righteousness of your Son. In Jesus name, I offer this prayer. Amen"

You believed in your heart and prayed. Now, believe that God accepted you and tell others about it. (Ro 10:9, 10) God doesn't lie. Read His word every day. Live according to His word. Now you can live the life of Christ since He is with you and in you. Praise the Lord!

SECTION II

Move into Christlikeness unhindered
Winds of teaching – tricky hindrances

Y ou turned to God. You set your eyes on Jesus and the Good News. You received the Gospel. You know for sure that you are saved. Praise the Lord! You long to go closer and closer to God. You look for help all around you. This is the experience of every believer who is saved by His grace. Various teachings on the Bible come handy to all. Here, now, a bit of caution. Jesus asks His disciples to be on their guard against the teachings of the Pharisees and Sadducees. Paul says that every teaching that comes handy is not safe as cunning and crafty men could be behind it. He says in Ephesians that we need not be tossed back and forth by the waves, and blown here and there by every wind of teaching and by the cunning and craftiness of men in their deceitful scheming. (Eph. 4:14). Those men want to have their say. Their desire is to make believers line up behind them. (Ac. 20:30 ; Gal. 4:17). There are some others who peddle the word of God for profit. They think godliness is a means to financial gain. (II Co. 2:17; I Ti. 6:5). Paul urges the believers, 'I urge you, brothers, to watch out for those who cause divisions and put obstacles in your way that are contrary to the teaching you have learned. Keep away from them. For such people are not serving our Lord Christ, but their own appetites. By smooth talk and flattery they deceive the minds of naive people.' (Ro. 16:17, 18). Peter confirms this by saying that there are some ignorant and unstable people who distort some of Paul's writings which are hard to understand. He calls them lawless men. (II Pe. 3:15-17).

Paul's struggle was with the Judaizers who were insisting that the believers should undergo circumcision and follow the Law to be saved. Paul was opposed to legalism. He explains, 'This matter arose because some false brothers had infiltrated our ranks to spy on the freedom we have in Christ Jesus and to make us slaves.' (Gal. 2:4). Paul says, 'In him you were also circumcised in the putting off of the sinful nature, not with a circumcision done by the hands of men but with the circumcision done by Christ.' (Col. 2:11). Those who were introducing Gnostic teaching were also confronted by Paul. They brought in, vain philosophy, mysticism and asceticism. He asks the Colossian believers not to be carried away by hollow and deceptive philosophy. He says that there are mystics who are puffed up by idle notions and ascetics who see virtue in forbidding certain things. He tells the believers that they should not allow these people to deprive them of their prize. He states that the believers have no need of all these because they died with Christ to the basic principles of this world. (Col 2:8, 18, 20, 21) All these were efforts to add something or another to 'the Cross of Christ' for salvation and Christian life.

The same efforts are seen even today in various forms. How do they do it? Is it by bringing teaching which is not in the Bible? No. They know you will surely detect. How, then? They pick one or two sentences out of the context to evolve their pet teaching. They make believers doubt time tested doctrines. They do not allow you to understand God's plan for your life from the truth presented in pairs. They use one or two incidents related to one or two characters in the Bible in their teaching. They leave one part of the story and connect unrelated events and challenge the believers. They make the believers tap only one means of grace leaving the rest. They make them put on only one piece of armour of God leaving the rest. They know that well-meaning believers fall into their trap, if Scripture is shown to them. You have good intentions. But they have set intentions to impose their teaching on you. Your intentions come to no effect when you receive their teaching. You need to have sound teaching to be able to detect and reject any false teaching that comes your way. You can obtain sound teaching only when you know first the ways in which you are to understand your Bible.

CHAPTER I

Principles of understanding the Bible

God speaks to His people through the Bible. The Bible is to be read time and again to hear from God. When you hear God's word you can understand His ways. He helps you to grow in your faith by speaking to you through the Bible every day. You need to be careful while reading the Bible as you have to understand it, the way, God wants you to understand it. There are some time tested principles which need to be noted while reading your Bible. The context of the portion of scripture; the syntax and grammar used; the literary style and the narrative details present and the time scale employed are all important. All these have to be taken into account to have a proper understanding of the Bible. All these serve as tools to get you closer to the meaning of the text.

Context

A very significant part of the Bible is narration. A narrative naturally contains a person, a place, a point of time and a situation. The best example of a narrative in the Bible is the Nativity of Christ: 'In the sixth month, God sent the angel Gabriel, to Nazareth, a town in Galilee to a virgin pledged to be married to a man named Joseph, a descendant of David. The virgin's name was Mary.' (Lk. 1:26, 27). We have Mary- a person, Nazareth- a place, sixth month- the time and 'pledged to be married to a man'- a situation. All narratives and other portions have a context. A context is the words that come before and after a particular word and it is the circumstances in which an event occurs. The context is very important to understand the meaning of a particular word used in a text.

'Faith' is a very important word in the Bible. Faith is the attitude whereby a man abandons all reliance on his own efforts to obtain salvation. It is the attitude of complete trust in Christ. It involves intellectual assent, commitment of the will and also reception in the heart. Faith does not stop with a person saying he believes that the Gospel is true. Faith is seen in a person's let going his self-will for God's will. Faith also enables a person to receive salvation and to say with certainty that he is saved. When a man comes to faith, he commits himself decisively to Christ. We see the determinative character of faith here. According to Paul, God justifies a person when He sees this faith. Faith here is considered unitary. It is measured as a single unit. '... It is by grace you have been saved, through faith - and this not from yourselves, it is the gift of God. -' (Eph. 2:8). Faith also shows itself as a continuing attitude. It is present faith which is continuous with a past act of belief. (I Co. 13:2). Matthew records, 'Then the disciples came to Jesus in private and asked, "Why couldn't we drive it out?" Jesus replied, "Because you have so little faith. I tell you the truth if you have faith as small as a mustard seed you can say to this mountain, 'Move from here to there' and it will move nothing will be impossible for you"' (Mt. 17:19, 20). This faith is also recorded in the eleventh chapter of Hebrews. We see here that this faith could be measured in degrees. It grows as more and more of God's word is received. It grows along with various kinds of God given experiences. Paul lists such faith as a gift. (I Co. 12:9).

Paul and James both use the word 'faith'. When Paul uses it in the context of justification, it is faith which is relying entirely on the finished work of Christ. When James uses it, in the context of works of a believer, it is different. It is the continuing attitude of faith, showing in warm deeds of love in complete reliance on God and full obedience to God.

According to Paul, God justifies a person when he accepts the Gospel in faith. People don't need to wait till they display the continuing attitude to receive salvation. Preachers challenging for such continuing attitude in faith to receive salvation, distort the Gospel. It is false teaching. The faith needed for salvation leads us to an instantaneous experience. God, like a judge, cancels the accusations on us and declares us righteous. It is a declaration. This may sound ridiculous to the world. Most religions believe in earning salvation by merit. That is no reason for us to shy away from preaching the Gospel. Paul states, 'I am not ashamed of the Gospel because it is the power of God for salvation of every one who believes: first for the Jew then for the Gentile.' (Ro. 1:16). It may sound as downplaying the righteousness to the world.

They do not know that God, only, began the good work in the person, who believed. He sends the Holy Spirit (The Spirit of His Son) into the heart of that person. Righteousness which hitherto eluded the believer becomes possible from now on. James challenges believers to show such righteousness in their life. This is possible. The Holy Spirit helps the believer to go on in his faith journey. When this order sounds so logical there are teachers who put the second aspect, the continuing attitude of faith, as the criterion for salvation. This leaves the aspirants struggling endlessly for salvation. This problem arises when the context of the word is ignored. The context of the word used is important while a teaching point is drawn.

In one of the discourses we see Jesus talking about good works. 'Then they asked him, "What must we do to do the works God requires?" Jesus answered, "the work of God is this: to believe in the one he has sent."' (Jn. 6:28, 29). If believing in Jesus is the work of God, religious piety and ethical good works cannot take the place of faith for justification. The word 'works' which Paul uses need not be confused with the same word with different stress which James uses. God's grace is not a thing to be bought with the merit of good works, any way!

Syntax and Grammar

Language is a system of words. Language conveys information. Every word in the Bible is important. Jesus says, 'I tell you the truth, until heaven and earth disappear, not the smallest letter, not the least of stroke of a pen, will by any means disappear from the Law until everything is accomplished.' (Mt. 5:18). We need to give importance to the syntax and grammar to know the meaning of the words. The context anyway is the overriding principle for complete understanding. Syntax is the way in which words are arranged to form phrases and sentences while grammar is the study of words and of the rules for their formation and their relationship to each other in sentences. In one of the discourses with the Jews, Jesus uses the sentence 'Before Abraham was born, I am!' The Jews rightly understood the meaning of the sentence by noting that Jesus purposefully violated grammar to make an 'I am' statement. Jesus used God's prerogative. Hence the Jews picked up stones. We understand from this that every stroke of a pen has meaning in God's word.

We can understand the meaning of the word 'salvation' fully if tenses employed are carefully noted. When Paul says we have been saved by grace, it is salvation possessively. It means we are declared righteous; we are freed from the penalty of sin. (Eph. 2:8). But when he says we are being saved, he means salvation is progressive. Here are his words: '... The message of the cross is foolishness to those who are perishing, but to us who are being saved it is the power of God.' (I Co. 1:18). It means we are being saved from the power of sin and attacks of Satan in this world, every day. Paul talks about salvation in futuristic terms as well. These are his words: '...Do this, understanding the present time. The hour has come for you to wake up from your slumber, because our salvation is nearer now than when we first believed.' (Ro. 13:11). When he says salvation is near, he means that our total redemption - deliverance from the very presence of sin - is in heaven. This is salvation expressed prospectively.

There are teachers who do not care for syntax and grammar in the text. They confuse believers and do not allow them to have assurance of salvation. The congregation is always kept on tenterhooks so far as their assurance of salvation is concerned. It limits their growth in the Lord. If what they do is right, what difference is there between religions which promise salvation at the time of death and Christianity? What they do is not right. There is a difference. We have eternal life now. We have the privilege of possessing the Spirit of His Son. We are privileged to be children of God right here in this world.

Literary style

Excepting a passage and a few words in Aramaic, the entire Old Testament is written in Hebrew. It is a language rich in imagery and poetic form. The New Testament is written in common Greek which enables graphic presentation. There are many occasions where writers in the Bible used imagery. It is the use of metaphoric language. This is with an intention to produce pictures in the minds of readers. This type of literature is intended to be clear to those who are receptive. It needs careful study. Interpretation is explaining the meaning of the text. We can gain access to the true meaning intended by the author by recognising the literary style employed in the text and by drawing careful interpretation. We may have to take either its literal meaning or its metaphoric meaning while interpreting the text. If figurative texts are interpreted literally and vice versa, there is always the danger of wrong interpretation.

There are many teachers who make use of the Song of Solomon to teach about love between Christ and the Church. God granted Solomon wisdom. It could be understood that God granted him all the possibilities in the world to study and understand human life. The Song could be taken as a treatise to present human love story in all its passion. Instead of understanding human love from a literal presentation in the Bible, if we allegorise it as love between the Church and Christ, there is every possibility for incorporating our ideas about the Church into the text.

There is the same danger if figurative texts in the book of Revelation are interpreted literally. The type of literature employed here, was intended primarily to be understood by those who had already been in touch with the author. It is our task to recover the realities which lie behind the imagery and symbolism involved. Teachers, who have a fancy for interpreting the book of Revelation, have been causing confusion in the minds of believers. The text is used for introducing all kinds of teaching which the teachers love to introduce. There are Churches which have their main doctrine based on imagery and symbolism present in the book of Revelation. How feeble this foundation is!

What is the need for allegorizing the Song of Solomon when there are other texts available for teaching the same concept? There are enough texts to speak about Jesus' love for the Church. In the light of teaching contained in the other books of the New Testament, we are to draw teaching from the allegorical presentation contained in the book of Revelation. There is no need for taking the material literally. Let us not give an opportunity to false teachers to have their say.

Narrative details

Narrations in the Bible contain many details. Wholesome understanding of the text becomes possible only when the details are given due importance. The book of Job is a single piece. The details in this book are summed up at the end. The story of the Samaritan woman in John chapter 4, the Blind man in John 9, conversion of the Ethiopian eunuch in Acts 8, the conversion of Cornelius, the centurion in Acts 10 and 11 etc. are events with many details. There is definite progress in the story in each one of these. When the order of development is given due importance, faltering in observation, interpretation and application of the Scripture is minimised.

Job is a book which has to be read completely before we make a comment on it. His friends are good men. They are knowledgeable persons. The words they utter are words of great wisdom. But why does God find fault with them? They did not respond the way they should respond to a situation. This, we can understand only at the end. Any teaching on the wisdom of Job's friends without reference to its conclusion is bound to be faulty. Now, we know that the suffering of Jesus on the cross brings solace to those who go through suffering. Jesus helps those who suffer as He himself went through suffering and death. (Heb. 2:17, 18). Now we know that the accuser of Job is a defeated foe.

Luke records in the Acts of the Apostles an event concerning the conversion of the Ethiopian eunuch. The Ethiopian eunuch had already been a worshipper of Jehovah. Evidently he was a proselyte. When He worshipped in the Jerusalem temple, God could have revealed Himself to him directly. The story continued. The reading of the Scripture became necessary. An evangelist had to give exposition of the Scripture portion. The story of the life and teaching of Jesus was not sufficient. The cross of Christ had to be preached. (Ro. 10:17). Then there was particularity in his faith. This led to his instantaneous salvation and also his very hour of baptism. False teachers are often guilty of the error of oversimplifying a concept. If someone says I believe in God and stops there, is it sufficient? It may sound good. But here is an error of oversimplification. May be he is trying deliberately to avoid details of salvation. God is God of generalities and also God of particularities. Jesus says, 'Trust in God; trust also in me'. (Jn. 14:1).

Long time ago I took a college student, into his hostel Chapel and explained to him in detail, the Gospel. To ensure whether he understood it or not, I put a question asking him what he should do to be saved. He said, "We should read the Bible and pray". Having thought that he did not understand the Gospel, I explained to him the importance of believing in Jesus Christ and his death on the cross for the forgiveness of our sins. I put my earlier question again. He gave the same answer. I tried again, saying that reading of the Bible and praying are important but believing the Gospel is all the more important for forgiveness of sins. I went into greater details. When I asked him the third time, his answer was exactly the one he gave first. Then I understood that he was deliberately rejecting the Gospel.

There is some such problem with regard to prayer as well. If someone teaches prayer as prayer to God and stops there, it is an error of oversimplification. Are not details for teaching on prayer available? We are asked to pray in the name of Jesus. If details are given due importance, we pray to the Father in the name of Jesus and in the Holy Spirit. Narrative details are important. In the Church history these details are given due importance. Now, we know why the Apostles Creed, which some parts of the Church confess every Sunday, runs into such great details. The members of the Church need to believe in these details to stay united.

Time scale

John came as a witness to testify concerning Jesus. He declared one day, 'I am the voice of one calling in the desert, "Make straight the way for the Lord"' (Jn. 1:23). 'The next day John saw Jesus coming toward him and said, "Look, the Lamb of God who takes away the sin of the world"' (Jn. 1:29). From the words of Jesus we understand that John is the last of the prophetical order. Jesus talked about a new era where the kingdom of God has been forcefully advancing. (Mt. 11:11-15). Jesus told them about the difference, in definite terms, during the forty days after His resurrection, '… John baptized with water, but in a few days you will be baptized with the Holy Spirit' (Ac. 1:5). Those days arrived. God's power was seen in the Gospel. People started rushing into the kingdom to the utter dismay of those who trust in the Law and their works. Paul said concerning these people, 'However to the man who does not work but trusts God, who justifies the wicked, his faith is credited as righteousness.' (Ro. 4:5). The trust of these people was on the death and resurrection of Jesus.

Jesus ushered people from the phase of John the Baptist to a new phase, the era of the Holy Spirit. Ignoring this, there are preachers today who talk at length on repentance preached by John the Baptist making it a merit for salvation. They have practically no time for speaking about the Gospel and God's grace. They challenge people taking the message text of John the Baptist. In the days of John the Baptist people were wondering about his person. 'The people were waiting expectantly and were all wondering in their hearts if John might possibly be the Christ.' (Lk. 3:15). Are not the preachers guilty of causing such confusion even today in the broad day light of the Gospel? John is not Christ. Jesus is Christ.

Jesus says, 'The time has come. The kingdom of God is near. Repent and believe in the good news!' (Mk. 1:15).Repentance is turning 180 degrees. It is needed. But repentance is not all that is needed. The Good News is to be believed. In the Acts of the Apostles we see Paul going round the world preaching the Good News. Finally the Gospel is 'all'. So, only this is needed. There are preachers who introduce the Law through the back door in the name of repentance. John the Baptist commanded the listeners to set things right. Can this alone earn salvation? Some preachers insist on restitution as a means for salvation. Is there not some possibility for boasting about restitution they made, ignoring the Good News? In such preaching there is no place for grace which is the only means for salvation. Further, we notice a change in Paul's approach while preaching the Gospel to the gentiles. Most often he merely welcomes them to believe in Jesus Christ.

There is another instance connected with 'time scale.' Jesus appeared to the disciples over a period of forty days after His resurrection. '… He gave them this command: "Do not leave Jerusalem, but wait for the gift my Father promised, which you have heard me speak about."' (Ac. 1:4). They went upstairs into the room where they were staying. They all joined together constantly in prayer. 'When the day of Pentecost came they were all together in one place. Suddenly a sound like the blowing of a violent wind came from heaven and filled the whole house where they were sitting. They saw what seemed to be tongues of fire that separated and came to rest on each one of them. They were all filled with the Holy Spirit and began to speak in other tongues as the Spirit enabled them.' (Ac. 2:1-4). This event took place at a definite point of time in the Bible. If we analyse it, we notice that there was a time Jesus was physically present with the disciples, a time when He was not present with them either physically or otherwise and a time when His presence was granted through the indwelling of the Holy Spirit on the day of Pentecost. There were definitely three stages in the sequence of events. (Jn. 16:16)

After this the Apostles and evangelists filled by the Holy Spirit went about preaching the Gospel. Preaching of the Gospel was a new development. They began speaking to people. The Gospel showed to people their state where they are without Christ and promised them a new state where they would be with Christ. The Gospel drew the line of separation. There were only two stages in their lives. When they accepted the Gospel they entered into a new state through the indwelling of the Holy Spirit. That is why the people were never asked to wait to receive the Holy Spirit. They received the Good News. Then they were filled with the Holy Spirit - sometimes with an outward sign and most other times without any outward sign. The most important statement was this: 'And the Lord added to their number daily those who were being saved.' We read about the conversion of the Ethiopian eunuch in Acts chapter 8, Cornelius in Acts 10 and Lydia and the Jailer in Acts 16. What is important in all these accounts is that the Holy Spirit led them into faith. After a person puts his faith in Jesus Christ and accepts the Gospel, he welcomes Jesus into his heart and receives the Holy Spirit. When the seekers questioned, 'What shall we do?', 'Peter replied, "Repent and be baptised, every one of you, in the name of Jesus Christ for the forgiveness of your sins. And you will receive the gift of the Holy Spirit. The promise is for you and your children and for all who are far off - for all whom the Lord our God will call."' (Ac. 2:38, 39). Peter does not speak about waiting for the Holy Spirit here. After all, the Holy Spirit is the one who brings conviction in the listeners at the outset! (Jn. 16:8).

Paul also says, '... You also were included in Christ when you heard the word of truth, the gospel of your salvation. Having believed, you were marked in him with a seal, the promised Holy Spirit,' (Eph. 1:13). He sees a natural consequence of faith - the indwelling of the Holy Spirit. (Ro. 5:5).There was meaning for the disciples waiting for the Holy Spirit in those historical circumstances. The event was unique as only the disciples had three stages in their faith life. Now we can have only two stages. Can we presently imagine a situation where Jesus is in the heart of a believer while the Holy Spirit is still to come? We cannot imagine. They are together always. What all we need now is to allow the Holy Spirit to have more and more control over our individual lives.

Conclusion

Usage of words in different contexts could mean differently. Noting the syntax and grammar is necessary for grasping the meaning of the sentences. Study of the literary style, makes you understand the intentions of the authors. Details of the text should be given importance as these lead you to the whole truth. When texts are presented in God's 'time scale' they are to be taken in their proper setting. This helps you to receive God's word in its proper perspective. All these make you understand the theme present in the writings.

CHAPTER II

Essential doctrines

I n common parlance 'doctrine' is a set of principles or beliefs held by a religious group. In the Old Testament 'doctrine' is something which is received. It is used in the sense of 'content of teaching' in the New Testament. Jesus talks about the origin of His teaching on one occasion. John records this in detail: 'The Jews were amazed and asked, "How did this man get such learning without having studied?" Jesus answered, "My teaching is not my own. It comes from him who sent me"' (Jn. 7:15, 16). Jesus contrasts His teaching with that of the teachers of the Law and the Pharisees. Jesus speaks about the origin of their teaching quoting God's word from Isaiah. Mathew records this: 'They worship me in vain; their teachings are but rules taught by men' (Mat. 15:9). Jesus talks to His disciples about the Pharisees and the Sadducees. '"Be careful," Jesus said to them. "Be on your guard against the yeast of the Pharisees and Sadducees." Jesus explains it to them. 'Then they understood that he was not telling them to guard against the yeast used in bread, but against the teaching of the Pharisees and Sadducees' (Mat.16:6, 12).

The disciples took note of the sayings of Jesus and began formulating Christian doctrine after Pentecost. God gave Paul revelation to understand His purposes. He interprets the events during the life time of Jesus and after His death and resurrection and puts these to writing. Jude calls this teaching and that of the other disciples, as the teaching which is once for all entrusted to the saints. (Jude 3). We cannot afford to add anything to it or subtract anything from it. The Church all along maintained it and contended for it. In the Church history we read about devout men like Athanasius who spent their life time on preserving the Biblical doctrine. The exhortations and cautions Paul gave to Timothy apply to all those who are saved by His grace. You need to be cautious on these essentials as they enable you to hold on to faith and good conscience.

There are certain essentials of Christian faith which are attacked time and again all along Church history. This is done often in a subtle way. There are attempts from within to lead believers astray by making them compromise. The enemy targets the foundations of the Christian faith. David says, '... Look, the wicked bend their bows; they set their arrows against the strings to shoot from the shadows at the upright in heart. When the foundations are being destroyed, what can the righteous do?' (Ps 11:2, 3). We need to be careful about the foundations. John says that we lose our reward if we compromise on the essential doctrine which is the teaching of Christ. (II Jn. 8, 9). In all essentials, God requires the Church to show unity of faith and to stand as one person. This is the foundation on which the superstructure could be built. Paul says, 'By the grace God has given me, I laid a foundation as an expert builder, and someone else is building on it. But each one should be careful how he builds.' (I Co. 3:10). If anybody falters on the person and work of Christ, his foundations are shaken. If we hold on to all doctrines which are essential, we save not only ourselves but also those who hear from us. (I Ti. 4:16). The following are some of the doctrines which cannot be compromised.

The Trinity

The Trinity is the three persons of the Godhead – the Father, the Son and the Holy Spirit. The word Godhead indicates divine nature.

The word 'Trinity' is not found in the Bible. It found its place in early Christian theology. It is implicit in the divine disclosure from the very beginning. It is the climactic formulation as a result of God's progressive revelation in human history. The Hebrew plural 'Elohim' for God and the mention of 'the Word' and 'the Spirit' at the time of creation laid the early foundation for the Trinity. (Ge. 1:1-3). At the baptism of Jesus in the Jordan, the presence of three persons can be distinctly seen: the Son being baptized, the Father speaking from heaven and the Spirit descending in the objective symbol of a dove. The disciples became curious about who He was. (Mk. 4:41).The disciples slowly learned to accept Jesus as the Second Person in the Trinity. (Mt. 14:33). Jesus asked them to trust also in Him (Jn. 14:1) and taught them to accept also the Holy Spirit as the Third Person. He said, '… I tell you the truth: It is for your good that I am going away. Unless I go away, the Counsellor will not come to you; but if I go, I will send him to you. When he comes, he will convict the world of guilt in regard to sin and righteousness and judgment' (Jn. 16:7, 8). When Jesus appeared to Thomas after His resurrection, 'Thomas said to him, "My Lord and my God!"' (Jn. 20:28). Then worship of the Second Person took a decisive form. Luke records, 'Then they worshiped him and returned to Jerusalem with great joy.' (Lk. 24:52). The experience of Pentecost made them accept the Holy Spirit as the Third Person. The baptismal formula given by Jesus in the great commission which includes the Holy Spirit launched them into the Trinitarian worship. The Apostolic benediction is a proof of their faith in the Triune God - one God in three persons. It takes the following form, 'May the grace of the Lord Jesus Christ, and the love of God, and the fellowship of the Holy Spirit be with you all' (II Co. 13:14). Thus the whole Church is led into unity of faith with regard to 'the Holy Trinity.'

Christian experience and life depend on the doctrine of the Trinity. God the Father chose us in Jesus Christ. It is His love. Through the blood of Jesus Christ we have redemption. We heard the word of truth, the Gospel. We believed in the Gospel of Jesus Christ and were marked in Him with a seal, the promised Holy Spirit. All three Persons are involved in our salvation. In the third century A.D, Arius refused to consider Jesus as co-equal to God the Father. Since then attempts to refuse the teaching of equality of Jesus with the Father have been made. There are sects which refuse to accept the doctrine of the Trinity. Those who do not accept this doctrine, fall out from Christian faith.

Those who show one person of the Trinity in conflict with the other two are treacherous. Those who cause confusion among the three persons make believers become uncertain. Those who teach on only one person impoverish the believers. In these days of specialisation in every field, there are teachers who specialise on only one person. Fellowship is built around that person. Some teach on the person and work of Christ and leave no room for teaching on the Father and the Holy Spirit. The Father is as important as the Son; so is the Holy Spirit. There is a wide spread campaign on the person and power of the Holy Spirit. The leaders are so very obsessed with power that they have no time to talk about the Father and the Son. This imbalance is the cause for the under-nourishment of the believers. (Jn. 16:14, 15). The competitive spirit in the preachers makes them feel as though there existed competition in the Godhead which is loathsome. They do it for temporary gain. False teachers resort to playing with the doctrine of the Trinity. We cannot call ourselves 'Christians' if we entertain different ideas on it. Some say we don't need to be bothered about the concept of the Trinity. Just because you do not understand it you cannot say that you are not bothered about it. It is a matter of concern. Accepting the doctrine of Trinity is fundamental to Christian faith.

Scripture - its purpose

The books which are acknowledged as canonical by the Church Fathers are together called the Bible. A term synonymous with 'The Bible' is 'The Writings' or 'The Scriptures.' These words are frequently used in the New Testament to denote the Old Testament documents in whole or in part. In the Hebrew Bible the books are arranged in three divisions- the Law, the Prophets and the Writings. This threefold division of the Hebrew Bible is reflected in the words of Jesus. 'He said to them, "This is what I told you while I was still with you: Everything must be fulfilled that is written about me in the Law of Moses, the Prophets and the Psalms"' (Lk. 24:44). Peter's words in his epistle give us an understanding of what the Scriptures contain. Concerning the letters of Paul, Peter says, 'He writes the same way in all his letters, speaking in them of these matters. His letters contain some things that are hard to understand, which ignorant and unstable people distort, as they do the other Scriptures, to their own destruction.' (II Pe. 3:16). Peter considers Paul's writings as part of the Scriptures. We can infer from his words that, the Scriptures consist of not only the Old Testament but also these- the Gospels, Acts of the Apostles, the Epistles and the book of Revelation.

Paul considers that all Scripture is God-breathed. He sees in it an overall purpose. He writes in his second letter to Timothy about the importance of the Scriptures. (IITi.3:15-17). According to Paul, the Holy Scriptures cause faith in Jesus Christ. Is it true? Does the Old Testament speak about, Jesus Christ? Yes. Now we know that the 'seed of woman' mentioned by God while talking to Eve is none other than Jesus. The prophet promised by God when the Israelites were afraid to listen to Him directly, is Jesus. Moses says, 'The LORD your God will raise up for you a prophet like me from among your own brothers. You must listen to him.' (Dt. 18:15). When David said, "The Lord said to my Lord," he clearly meant that Jesus is his Lord. Jesus proved it on one occasion. (Lk. 20:41-44). On another occasion Philip told Nathanael that he found Jesus as the one about whom Moses and the prophets wrote. (Jn. 1:45). The prophets prophesied concerning Jesus and Jesus fulfilled them. Isaiah, chapter 53 looks like a record of a journalist, on the day of crucifixion, in Jerusalem. Matthew recorded stage by stage how the Old Testament prophesies were fulfilled in Jesus Christ. So the Scriptures reveal Jesus Christ. These Scriptures by revealing Jesus Christ draw man into faith in Him. Paul says, 'Consequently, faith comes from hearing the message, and the message is heard through the word of Christ.' (Ro. 10:17). God chose it this way. He attributed power to God's word to generate faith in the hearers. It is clearly seen from the story of the rich man and Lazarus. When the rich man pleaded with Abraham to send Lazarus from the dead saying that his brothers, then only would repent, "He said to him, 'If they do not listen to Moses and the Prophets, they will not be convinced even if someone rises from the dead" (Lk. 16:31). It shows God's appointed place for the Scriptures in drawing man into faith in Jesus Christ. God's word convinces people- not supernatural demonstrations. These draw people to God's word only. God's word imparts faith. According to Paul, that faith leads man to salvation. Only the Scripture is useful, all along his way to a believer, in this world.

God expects everyone to receive His word from the Bible. All of us need to be united in accepting the entire Bible as His word. There are those who say that the Bible contains God's word. What do they mean? Which is the other word? Who decides which part is God's word and which is not? The west-minister confession of faith lists the thirty nine books of the Old Testament and twenty seven books of the New Testament as all given by the inspiration of God, to be the rule of faith and life. Peter, concerning the Scripture, leaves no room for speculation. He says, 'Above all, you must understand that no prophecy of Scripture came about by the prophet's own interpretation. For prophecy never had its origin in the will of man, but men spoke from God as they were carried along by the Holy Spirit.' (II Pe. 1:20, 21). False teachers attack the minds of believers. They know that once doubt is created in the minds of believers, any teaching they want to introduce will easily be received by them. How zealous they are for promoting their teaching! How blessed we will be if we take the whole Bible as God's word spoken by men who were inspired by the Holy Spirit!

Universal sinfulness

God created man on the sixth day in His image and likeness. Man is the crown of God's creation. God's purpose is to make man rule over the earth. These are His words concerning the creation of man, "Let us make man in our image and in our likeness". (Ge. 1:26). The image of God could best be understood as his freedom. In his own freedom man could either obey God or disobey. God commanded man not to eat the fruit of the tree of knowledge of good and evil. This is to make man test his own freedom. Disobedience is the violation of the command of God and it is repudiation of His authority. Satan prompted him to disobey. Man disobeyed. Man fell into sin and God's curse came upon him. Sin brought a change in man's attitude towards God. The first sin of Adam had unique significance for the whole human race. Paul says, 'Therefore, just as sin entered the world through one man, and death through sin, and in this way death came to all men, because all sinned.' (Ro. 5:12). Why is he imputing sin to all men? It is because he sees the sin of all mankind in the sin of Adam.

There is a case presented by the writer to the Hebrews which can convince us to have such an understanding. The writer to the Hebrews, to prove his point that Jesus is the Great High Priest, says, that Abraham gave a tenth part of all to Melchizedek. He says that Jesus is like Melchizedek who is without genealogy. The writer's argument is that when Abraham gave a tenth to Melchizedek, it amounts to saying that Levi also gave the tenth. These are his words: 'One might even say that Levi, who collects the tenth, paid the tenth through Abraham, because when Melchizedek met Abraham, Levi was still in the loins of his ancestor' (Heb. 7:9, 10). Basing on this argument we can accept that when the first Adam sinned, the entire human race was present in him. Hence the imputation of sinfulness to all humanity is proper and justifiable.

There are teachers who want to express their humanism. They express their sympathy for human beings by rejecting the doctrine of universal sinfulness of man. They insist on the adequacy of created human nature- essentially unimpaired by Adam's fall- to fulfil the will of God. They deny original sin. They fall in line with Pelagius a teacher of Christian asceticism in the early fifth century A.D, who propounded this theory. Those who do not speak of universal sinfulness deprive us of 'our identification with Adam'- the true humanness; and lead us astray. We become blind to notice the governing principle of salvation through the blood of Jesus Christ. If this principle is ignored by anyone, there remains no hope for him. Paul explains that one sin of Adam brought death on mankind. He says that God's grace through Jesus Christ, the 'Last Adam', brought justification and life to all those who believe. (Ro. 5:14-19). In faith we opt out from the first Adam and join the 'Last Adam'. It is like jumping into a life boat from a sinking ship. We have life everlasting in Jesus. The 'Last Adam' Jesus is our fountain head.

Virgin birth - the incarnation

The word 'Virgin' is the translation of a Hebrew word which means 'to separate.' Matthew and Luke tell the story about the virgin birth of Jesus. Luke records it like this: "'How will this be," Mary asked the angel, "Since I am a virgin?" The angel answered, "The Holy Spirit will come upon you, and the power of the Most High will overshadow you. So the holy one to be born will be called the Son of God'" (Lk. 1:34, 35). Matthew records it from the point of view of Joseph. The angel asks Joseph not to be afraid of taking Mary as his wife, and tells him that what is conceived in her is from the Holy Spirit. (Mt 1:18, 20). Matthew records it to make it known to the Jews and Luke records it to make it known to the Gentiles. We don't find the mention of virgin birth elsewhere in the New Testament since the aim of the authors was never to dissect the mystery of His person. It was not needed again as their concern was to show only the relation of Jesus to the saving purposes of God. It was enough for them to proclaim incarnation as a fact. We can draw a parallel between the sinlessness of the incarnate Son Jesus and the sinlessness of Adam before his fall. Paul presents Jesus as 'the Last Adam'. Jesus was born sinless as the first Adam was created sinless. The first Adam though created sinless fell into temptation and brought sin and death on himself and on the entire mankind. 'The Last Adam', Jesus, though tempted the same way, did not fall into temptation. He overcame temptation and brought righteousness and life to mankind. The apostolic writers clearly see that both the deity and manhood of Jesus are fundamental to His saving work.

The Apostle Paul quotes a hymn on the incarnation of Jesus to prove this point. (I Ti. 3:16). It shows the deity and manhood of Jesus. Jesus, at Caesarea Philippi put before the disciples, the puzzle on His person and made them to have a glimpse of God's revelation on His deity. He asks them to tell him who, the people say, He is. After they give various answers, He asks them to tell Him who, they personally say, He is. Peter confesses that Jesus is the Christ, the Son of the Living God. (Mt.16:13-17; 20). Soon after this, He talked about His death to make them understand that He is fully man as He is fully God. When the records present Him fully as man, it appears to us as though He was not God. When they present Him fully as God, they make us feel as though He was not man. Jesus was born as a baby. He was to be protected by Joseph. He grew as a boy of great understanding. 'Everyone who heard him was amazed at his understanding and his answers.' '… Jesus grew in wisdom and stature, and in favour with God and men' (Lk. 2:47, 52). Jesus asked for baptism as any other Jew did. (Mt. 3:13-15). Jesus was tired. John records, 'Jacob's well was there, and Jesus, tired as he was from the journey, sat down by the well. It was about the sixth hour.' (Jn.4:6). He was hungry. Mark records, 'The next day as they were leaving Bethany, Jesus was hungry.' (Mk.11:12). He fell fast asleep. Mark records, 'Jesus was in the stern, sleeping on a cushion. The disciples woke him and said to him, "Teacher, don't you care if we drown?"' (Mk. 4:38). He was thirsty. John records, 'Later, knowing that all was now completed, and so that the Scripture would be fulfilled, Jesus said, "I am thirsty"' (Jn. 19:28).

All these records present Jesus fully as a man. But there are other records which show otherwise. He used the language which is God's prerogative. He used an "I am" Statement. "I tell you the truth," Jesus answered, "before Abraham was born, I am!" At this, they picked up stones to stone him, but Jesus hid himself, slipping away from the temple grounds.' (Jn. 8:58, 59). He differed with the Jews on his identity. They said, "'… We know where this man is from; when the Christ comes, no one will know where he is from." Then Jesus, still teaching in the temple courts, cried out, "Yes, you know me, and you know where I am from. I am not here on my own, but he who sent me is true. You do not know him, but I know him because I am from him and he sent me."' (Jn. 7:27-29). He forgave sins. Mark records, 'When Jesus saw their faith, he said to the paralytic, "Son, your sins are forgiven."' (Mk. 2:5). He made known His authority. According to Mark, Jesus declares, "'But that you may know that the Son of Man has authority on earth to forgive sins…."' (Mk. 2:10). So Jesus is both man and God at the same time. It is because He is man His sacrificial death is of avail. It is because He is God His forgiveness of sins is of avail.

There are some who say that they do not believe in the virgin birth. Do they mean to say that the Bible contains some fairy tales as well? There are others who speak light of incarnation. They want to please the Eastern philosophers who believe that man can attain perfection one day. The philosophers say that Jesus is mere man who at a point of time in His life attained perfection. They say that there are others who had already attained perfection. The Bible teachers, who compromise on this, teach the Bible on human terms. John ascribes to the spirit of antichrist any denial that Jesus Christ is come in the flesh. He says, 'this is how you can recognize the Spirit of God: Every spirit that acknowledges that Jesus Christ has come in the flesh is from God, but every spirit that does not acknowledge Jesus is not from God. This is the spirit of the antichrist, which you have heard is coming and even now is already in the world.' (I Jn. 4:2, 3). He continues, 'Many deceivers, who do not acknowledge Jesus Christ as coming in the flesh, have gone out into the world. Any such person is the deceiver and the antichrist.' (II Jn. 7).

Resurrection

Resurrection is rising from the dead. 'Resurrection of Jesus Christ from the dead' is a constituent of the gospel. Paul says, '... What I received I passed on to you as of first importance: that Christ died for our sins according to the Scriptures, that he was buried, that he was raised on the third day according to the Scriptures.' (I Co. 15:3, 4). In the final analysis, forgiveness of sins depends also on the fact of resurrection. Paul puts before the Corinthian believers his logical argument in the reverse when they begin doubting the resurrection of the dead. He reasons that Christ is not raised if there is no resurrection of the dead; if He is not raised, he says that their preaching about His resurrection is a lie. He concludes saying that if such a lie is believed, their faith is futile and they remain in their sins. (I Co. 15:14-17). He makes them to come to their senses. He wants them to cast their doubts aside and believe first in the resurrection of Jesus Christ.

Our Lord appeared over a period of some weeks to His followers. Further the tomb remained empty. The allegation that the disciples stole away the body is as old as the event. Matthew records, 'When the chief priests had met with the elders and devised a plan, they gave the soldiers a large sum of money, telling them, "You are to say, 'His disciples came during the night and stole him away while we were asleep.' If this report gets to the governor, we will satisfy him and keep you out of trouble." So the soldiers took the money and did as they were instructed. And this story has been widely circulated among the Jews to this very day.' (Mt. 28:12-15). The disciples took to their heels at the time of crucifixion. The story that they stole the body with an intention to proclaim His resurrection would sound ridiculous to everybody that time. Supposing his followers went to the wrong tomb, would not the Jews bring out the body from the right tomb to prove that He did not rise? If someone says that it was mere hallucination, our question is, 'could it occur to such large number of people at one time?' No. Hallucination is not true. Paul challenges those who say He is not raised by listing His appearances along with the one in which more than five hundred saw him at one time. He says it could be verified from many of those who were alive still. Paul presents the proofs on the resurrection of Jesus Christ and talks at length on resurrection of the dead which is its corollary. The resurrection is of very first importance for Christian faith. The first preachers were sure that Christ had risen, and equally sure that, in consequence, the believers would also rise in due course. (I Co. 6:14). What a wonderful hope for the believers in the face of the inevitability of death!

There are preachers who leave some doubt by saying that they are not bothered about what happened that day and say that He is anyway resurrected in their hearts. What are we to infer from such statements? Our faith stands or falls on the fact of resurrection. Such preachers cause believers to stumble in their faith. Some talk about Christ of the cosmos and leave out Jesus of Nazareth to please people from other faiths. These people have no problem in accepting that Christ of the cosmos- the Universal Spirit - pervades the universe. How will it help these people when it is not the Gospel? Such all - inclusive faith leads all to the broad way; the end of it is destruction. The Gospel includes bodily resurrection of Jesus Christ. We believe the Gospel. Jesus is risen! 'He is risen indeed' is our response.

Holy Spirit – His presence in the life of a believer

The Holy Spirit is referred to as 'Holy Ghost,' 'Spirit,' 'Spirit of God,' 'Spirit of Christ,' and 'the comforter' in the Bible. He is the Third Person in the Holy Trinity. We see that the Holy Spirit is at work both in the Old Testament and in the New Testament just as the Father and the Son are at work. But in the Old Testament, we see Him work more as a force than as a person. In the New Testament awareness of the Holy Spirit as a person is gradually built. Whether it was in the Old Testament or in the New Testament, the work was God's power all along. In the Old Testament God's power was made available to Gideon. The Spirit of the LORD came upon Gideon. (Jdg. 6:34). It happened the same way with Samson. (Jdg. 15:14). When Saul was to be made King, he too experienced the power of God. (I Sa. 11:6). The Holy Spirit inspired the prophets to prophesy the immediate, near and far off future events. He inspired the prophets to foretell the arrival of the Messiah. The power of the Holy Spirit was seen in the virgin birth of Christ.

After Jesus was born, we notice the presence of the Holy Spirit only at the time of His baptism. The Holy Spirit descended on Him like a dove. We do not hear much about the Holy Spirit later. In the presence of the incarnate Son, the small number of disciples around Him received all the comfort and counsel through the Son. Only when He was to leave, we hear of the need of the Holy Spirit, another comforter. So Jesus explained to them the person-hood of the Holy Spirit. Ezekiel prophesied about the indwelling of the Spirit. It is God's promise. God said, '... I will put my Spirit in you and move you to follow my decrees and be careful to keep my laws' (Eze. 36:27). These are the words of Jesus about the Holy Spirit: "'If you love me, you will obey what I command. And I will ask the Father, and he will give you another Counsellor to be with you forever - the Spirit of truth. The world cannot accept him, because it neither sees him nor knows him. But you know him, for he lives with you and will be in you.'" (Jn. 14:15-17). He is none other than 'the Spirit of God', also called 'the Spirit of Christ.' (Jn. 14:23). These promises were fulfilled on the day of Pentecost.

David foresaw the role of the Holy Spirit and expressed his longing for moral living: 'Search me, O God, and know my heart; test me and know my anxious thoughts. See if there is any offensive way in me, and lead me in the way everlasting.' (Ps. 139:23, 24). God's promise of the indwelling Spirit in the book of Ezekiel is primarily to see that they follow His decrees and keep His laws. Paul talks about such life through the Spirit in his epistles. (Ro. 8:9-11).

There are some who do not recognise the Holy Spirit as a person. There are others who do not believe in the indwelling of the Holy Spirit.

The only difference the new covenant brings about in the believer is the indwelling of the Holy Spirit in his life. This has become possible because of the death and resurrection of Jesus Christ. If this is not accepted we fall out from the unity of faith and we have no place in the new covenant. It amounts to saying that we have not received the gift of salvation. The presence of the Holy Spirit is the hall mark of a believer. Paul draws this as the dividing line- the line of separation. He says, 'If any one does not have the Spirit of Christ he does not belong to Christ.'(Ro. 8:9).

The Church – 'called out' and separate

The English word 'Church' means 'The Lord's house' or a Christian place of worship. For the first Jewish Christians it was, 'God's people called together'. The emphasis was always on people. For them no separate words were needed for local congregation and congregations everywhere. Paul also doesn't use two separate words. He says that God placed all things under the feet of Jesus and appointed Him to be head over everything for the Church, which is his body. (Eph. 1:22, 23). Paul doesn't use the word 'Churches' for all the individual congregations put together. (Eph. 3:10). The one 'Church' was not an amalgamation or federation of the many. It is a heavenly reality, whether it is local or universal. Paul considers the 'Church' as a family, which also includes those who had already finished the race. Paul states, 'For this reason I kneel before the Father, from whom his whole family in heaven and on earth derives its name.' (Eph. 3:14, 15).

Peter's confession of Christ at Caesarea Philippi is the key event which lays the foundation for the Christian concept of the Church. (Mt. 16:18, 19). In the light of many scriptural portions we can conclude that the rock mentioned by Jesus is 'the confession' that Jesus is the Christ. The following portions of Scripture present Jesus Christ as the foundation of the Church. Paul says, '… No one can lay any foundation other than the one already laid, which is Jesus Christ' (I Co. 3:11). Peter received God's revelation. So he knew what Jesus meant when He called him Peter and he quoted from Psalms in support of it. (Ac. 4:11). In his epistles he makes it all the more clear. (I Pe. 2:6-8).

The Church is the assembly of called out people. Peter says, '... You are a chosen people, a royal priesthood, a holy nation, a people belonging to God, that you may declare the praises of him who called you out of darkness into his wonderful light.' (I Pe.2:9). Jesus in His high priestly prayer draws a clear distinction between those whom the Father gave Him and the rest. Jesus prays, "'My prayer is not for them alone. I pray also for those who will believe in me through their message, that all of them may be one, Father, just as you are in me and I am in you. May they also be in us so that the world may believe that you have sent me.'" (Jn. 17:20, 21). He says that they are in the world. He draws a line of separation between them and the world by saying that they are not of the world.

However much pain the division may cause to the champions for the good of the world, the claims of Jesus cannot be changed. They are exclusive claims. Truth is truth. But the love of Jesus is all inclusive. There are preachers who do not want to draw a line of distinction between the saved and the unsaved in the congregation. As generations pass and as children, grandchildren and great grandchildren attend the service, meaning of 'called out' is ignored. They do not like to preach on repentance and salvation. Born again experience is an unnecessary concept for them. John in his prologue on the Word emphasises the difference between God's children and the rest of the world. He says, 'He was in the world, and though the world was made through him, the world did not recognize him. He came to that which was his own, but his own did not receive him. Yet to all who receive him, to those who believed in his name, he gave the right to become children of God- children born not of natural descent, nor of human decision or a husband's will, but born of God.' (Jn. 1:10-13). Children or grandchildren each one is a person before God, created in His image. Everyone should receive born again experience to become a child of God- the 'called out' into His family.

There is a tradition which confers authority to the Church over the Scriptures. People are asked to receive the word as interpreted by the Church as God's word. How can it be possible? The Church is to be subjected to the word of God. The Church can never be above God's word. The word of the One who called is higher than the people who are called. The Church is to interpret the Scripture in obedience to the authority of the Scripture.

In the midst of pluralistic religions, the Church is to exist with a desire to work along with Jesus to bring in others. Jesus says, 'I have other sheep that are not of this sheep pen. I must bring them also. They too will listen to my voice, and there shall be one flock and one shepherd.' (Jn. 10:16). The line of separation between the saved and the unsaved, changes each time when Gospel is received by others. When we meet someone our attitude should be this: 'I am a saved person today. He may be a saved person very soon.' The Church exists for others. God loves every one. (Jn. 3:16).

Second Coming - the timing

In the Old Testament 'the Day of the Lord' indicates the visit of the God of Israel with the purpose of judging the wicked and redeeming the righteous. It is a single day. Joel exclaims, 'Alas for that day! For the day of the LORD is near; it will come like destruction from the Almighty.' (Joel. 1:15). Amos warns, 'Woe to you who long for the day of the LORD! Why do you long for the day of the LORD? That day will be darkness, not light.' (Amos 5:18). But in the New Testament 'the Day of the Lord' is split into two. Someone says it is like viewing two mountain peaks from a long distance. The two peaks appear as one from there. People in the Old Testament saw it as one peak- one day. People in the New Testament are like those who are in the valley between the peaks. For them these are two-one at the back and another in the front. The New Testament sees in the incarnation of Christ the fulfilment of the Old Testament hope. It is one day. The other day is the day of consummation. Fulfilment and consummation are two parts of the redemptive work of God. 'The last days' which establish the Kingdom of God are now here. (Heb. 1:2). The Kingdom of God has already begun. Paul declares, '… He has rescued us from the dominion of darkness and brought us into the kingdom of the Son he loves.' (Col. 1:13). We are in God's Kingdom- the Christ centred rule of God. The day of consummation is ahead. It is the day of His coming again.

It is evident that the Second Coming of Christ occurs basically in two stages. In stage I, Christ comes for His own. The believing people are caught up to meet Him in the air. In stage II, Christ comes with His own. He comes with His saints to the earth. There may be a considerable length of interval between these two stages. If we accept that there is an interval, many difficult portions on tribulation in the book of Revelation or elsewhere could be understood with ease. A succession of events follows His coming to the earth. A careful study of Scriptures may enable us to approximately frame an order for the future events.

The 'Second Coming of Christ' was an event of great curiosity and concern for the disciples of Jesus. Matthew records, 'As Jesus was sitting on the Mount of Olives, the disciples came to him privately. "Tell us," they said, "When will this happen, and what will be the sign of your coming and of the end of the age?"' (Mt. 24:3). Jesus talked to them on the events prior to His coming at length. He told them that they would hear of wars and rumours of wars; nation would rise against nation, and kingdom against kingdom; there would be famines and earthquakes in various places. (Mt. 24:4-8). The Second Coming of Jesus Christ is an event which is taught in the epistles with certainty. Paul says that the Lord himself will come down from heaven, with a loud command, with the voice of the archangel and with the trumpet call of God bringing along with Him the dead in Christ. He adds that we who are still alive and are left will be caught up together with them in the clouds. (I Th. 4:13-18).

There are attempts to misguide believers on the Second Coming. There are Bible teachers who erroneously teach that the death of a believer itself is the Second Coming. There are others who say that the coming of the Holy Spirit on the day of Pentecost was the Second Coming of Christ. There are some others who emphasise symbolic Second Coming rather than literal Second Coming. The book of Revelation is the key book on the Second Coming. It contains along with narration, imageries and symbolisms. There are two extreme positions taken on the book of Revelation. Some teachers view at it as a completely symbolic literature which has no purpose in the present. They cause the believers to skip it. There are others who teach it completely as literal material. Those teachers, who skip the book of Revelation deliberately, aim at making "Second Coming" a non-event in human history. The latter group bring in whole lot of unbiblical speculation. Revelation is a book which emphasises the imminence of the Second Coming.

Speculation on the day of His coming is widely promoted. But Jesus tells His disciples, 'No one knows about that day or hour, not even the angels in heaven, nor the Son, but only the Father.' (Mt. 24:36). There is extensive teaching in the Bible on the Second Coming of Christ exclusively to bring about watchfulness on the part of the faithful. Jesus says, 'Therefore keep watch, because you do not know on what day your Lord will come' (Mt. 24:42). Paul says, 'Now, brothers, about times and dates we do not need to write to you, for you know very well that the day of the Lord will come like a thief in the night.' 'So then, let us not be like others, who are asleep, but let us be alert and self-controlled.' (I Th. 5:1, 2, 6). The Lord's coming is sure. Our job is to be alert. Each day of our life is purposeful. False teachers are on the increase. They have no time for the Gospel. They want to demonstrate their expertise on the subject of the Second Coming. Let no false teacher detract us. Maranatha!

Conclusion

Paul calls for unity in the Body of Christ. He says, 'Make every effort to keep the unity of the Spirit through the bond of peace.' (Eph. 4:3). He says that there is one faith, one body and one Spirit. Paul urges Ephesian believers to work for reaching unity in this faith. Unity in faith is possible if we receive the apostolic teaching. Our faith is that God is one-one God in three persons. The person and work of Jesus Christ is of meaning to us because we accept the universality of sinfulness. We believe in the Virgin birth and that God sent His Son to deliver us from sin. The Gospel in which we believe includes the death and also resurrection of Jesus Christ. The Holy Spirit indwells us as we wait as His called out people - the Church, for the coming of Christ. We also believe that Jesus will come again to judge the quick and the dead. The basis for all this is our faith in the inerrant and infallible word of God. The Apostles Creed contains the essential doctrines.

It runs like this. "I believe in God the Father Almighty, Maker of heaven and earth. And in Jesus Christ his only Son our Lord, who was conceived by the Holy Spirit, Born of the virgin Mary, suffered under Pontius Pilate, was crucified dead and buried, He descended into hell; the third day He rose again from the dead, He ascended into heaven, and sitteth on the right hand of God the Father Almighty; from thence He shall come to judge the quick and the dead. I believe in the Holy Spirit; the Holy Catholic Church, the communion of saints; the forgiveness of sins; the resurrection of the body; and the life everlasting. Amen."

CHAPTER III

Truth in pairs

M oses put before the Israelites only two options- life and death. Joshua challenged Israelites to choose between the Lord and the other gods to serve. Jeremiah also spoke of two ways. Jesus, in the 'Sermon on the Mount' asks them to enter through the narrow gate leaving only one option- the broad gate. He talks about only two trees- the good tree and the bad tree. He compares the one who hears His words and puts them into practice to a wise man who built his house on a rock. He compares the one who hears His words and does not put them into practice to a foolish man who built his house on sand. John in his gospel contrasts one with the other- light with darkness; life with death; truth with lie; belief with disbelief etc. In all these we are to choose one and leave out the other. Here we can draw a line of separation between the two. One of the two in the pair excludes the other. It has an exclusive nature.

There are pairs of truth in the Bible in which each one complements the other. You understand the implications of each one only when you study the other. Sound understanding becomes possible only when both are taken for study. You cannot afford to take one and leave out the other, according to your convenience. You understand God's plan for your life from the truth presented in pairs. Any teaching basing itself on only one of these two is bound to be erroneous. When such teaching is practised and promoted by some teachers with vigour you tend to believe it- if you receive only from them. Truth becomes worse than a lie not only when anything is added but also when anything is left out. You need to have it in full to be balanced in all areas of your life.

Objective truth and Subjective experience

God of the Bible exists outside a person's mind. There are very few religions in the world which believe that God is an objective reality. Many other religions believe in reality which exists in a person's mind and not produced by things outside it. For them, man is a subjective reality and also the ultimate reality. But the God of the Bible is an objective reality. God is God irrespective of man recognizing His existence or not. He is transcendental - wholly the other. Yet He is immanent - all pervading.

God chose to enable His creation – man, to experience His reality subjectively. 'For this is what the High and Lofty one says, He who lives forever, whose name is holy: "I live in a high and holy place, but also with him who is contrite and lowly in spirit to revive the spirit of the lowly and to revive the heart of the contrite"' (Isa. 57:15). God made the experience of His reality to human beings possible by sending His Son Jesus Christ into the world. Jesus revealed God to man. God arranged for man's forgiveness of sins in the sacrificial death of His Son. He completed the work of salvation before offering it. Hence His Gospel of salvation cannot have any human element in it. His covenant is either accepted or rejected. This objective reality makes acceptance necessary. The transcendental God becomes his "Immanuel" if Gospel is accepted by man.

Truth about God is presented extensively in the Bible. It absorbs our mind when we study it. It gives us great delight if we grapple with this truth. There are Bible scholars who have become very popular by their scholarship. They talk at length on objective reality. If they delight only in the truth about God while ignoring to enjoy the experience of salvation, they are the losers. The ultimate purpose of the Biblical revelation is salvation of men. We need to relate ourselves with God as a son relates himself with his father. Paul states, 'Because you are sons God sent the Spirit of his Son into our hearts, the Spirit who calls out, *"Abba*, Father"' (Gal. 4:6).

On the other hand if we are obsessed only with our personal experience paying little attention to reading His word objectively to enjoy His truth, are we not also the losers? There are preachers who talk all the time about experience. They make believers long for experience. Once I heard a conversation between two believers. The younger believer was saying that the entire Bible is God's word. The other disagreed with that; and stated saying that the word which glows in the heart of a believer is God's word to him. He was unable to convince the younger one as he was able to see the Bible objectively as God's word. God's word is God's word irrespective of a man recognising it or not. (ITh. 2:13). The truth about God is the basis for any experience. We can love God or worship God only to the extent we know about Him. (Jer. 23:23, 24). God's word makes us know more and more about what He is and what He wants from us. He is to be objectively viewed at before we subjectively know Him. Hence objective truth and subjective experience both are to be held in tension for balanced Christian living.

Sovereignty of God and Human responsibility

God is omniscient, omnipresent and omnipotent. He has sovereign power. God's power is His creative attribute. God's will expresses His self-determination. God has the power to carry out His purposes. This is called Sovereignty of God. Sovereignty is attributed to Him in the prayers of Nehemiah, Daniel and others. Daniel praises God after God revealed to him the meaning of the dream of the king. He says, 'Praise be to the name of God for ever and ever; wisdom and power are his. He changes times and seasons; he sets up kings and deposes them. He gives wisdom to the wise and knowledge to the discerning.' (Da. 2:20, 21)

Adam was created in the image and likeness of God. He is given freedom. In freedom he can choose either to obey God or disobey. Adam exercised his freedom only to disobey and ate the fruit. God put probing questions to Adam and Eve to make them feel accountable.

Man becomes accountable for his deeds. God asks Cain, "where is your brother Abel?" Cain replies, "I don't know. Am I my brother's keeper?" Since then human responsibility, in the light of divine sovereignty has been questioned. But Jesus in His earthly life demonstrated in His relationship with His father, the perfect blending of divine sovereignty and human responsibility. The choice of Jacob and Pharaoh by God for opposite purposes is discussed by Paul. Paul displaying his communicative skills puts to himself a hypothetical question from the readers. He says, 'One of you will say to me: "Then why does God still blame us? For who resists his will?"' (Ro. 9:19) Paul recognises the need to reconcile God's sovereignty and human responsibility. He deals with it at length. He sees God's sovereignty in the choice of Israel and human responsibility in the unbelief of Israel. (Ro. Chs.9, 10 & 11)

'Predestination' is the doctrine which states that God has foreordained all that happens. But it cannot relieve man of his responsibility. To understand 'predestination' we need to consider the nature of divine knowledge and His comprehension of all the Laws that govern human conduct. Some monotheistic religions go to one extreme and say that God is sovereign and man is only what God wills him to be. Some Eastern religions go to the other extreme and make man the ultimate authority to carry out his own purposes. But Christianity is a blending of God's sovereignty and human responsibility. It is true that God predestined some. If it is because of His foreknowledge that they would eventually believe in the Gospel, His grace loses its value and man gains a point here for boasting. If the doctrine of predestination rules out the freedom of choice, the Gospel loses its meaning. Those who teach it make believers lose their urge to preach the Gospel in urgency. Predestination and human freedom are both Biblical. They are to be held together. Certainly it is a mystery.

This can be traced in individual lives. Sovereignty of God is seen in His hating Esau and choosing Jacob. But Esau's responsibility remained. He is blamed for selling his birth right. We notice that Pharaoh had already been wicked with the Israelites before God hardened his heart. He cannot escape responsibility. Jesus talks about the son of perdition, Judas, 'The Son of Man will go just as it is written about him. But woe to that man who betrays the Son of Man! It would be better for him if he had not been born.' (Mk. 14:21). What does it mean? It speaks of God's sovereignty and at the same time human responsibility. Judas cannot escape from the responsibility of his deed, saying that it was any way destined. His deliberate choice is seen there. Why should Judas opt for doing it? God any way would accomplish His purposes. It is true that 'The LORD works out everything for his own ends - even the wicked for a day of disaster.' (Pr. 16:4). Why should Judas or anybody volunteer to be categorised in the general list of 'the wicked'? Further, God's purposes are not, primarily, to send some to hell and some to heaven. We see that God's purposes are different. The loftiest desire of God in the life of any person is to make him conform to the image of His Son. (Ro. 8:29). Hence God's sovereignty and human responsibility are to be held in tension. Both are Biblical. We celebrate the mystery. Secrets belong to the Lord!

Law and Grace

The first five books of the Bible contain ceremonial, ethical, social and other laws. The divine origin of these laws is stressed nearly everywhere in the Bible. The written "Torah" was to be guarded by the priests at the sanctuary. David always delighted in the Law of the Lord. (Ps. 119:97-104). Paul sees in the Law, the expression of God's will. He makes a series of positive comments on the role of Law (Ro.ch.7): it is the Law which made him know what sin is; it is the Law which pointed to him that coveting was sin (v.7ff); the intention of the Law is to bring life (v.10ff); the Law is holy, and the commandment is holy, righteous and good (v.12); the Law is spiritual (v.14). God's Law is delight to the eyes. How wonderfully it dissects the life of people! It makes people know what they lack. It creates deep desire in man for salvation.

It pleases people to work their way for salvation by fulfilling the Law. If they aim at it, it gratifies them to challenge others to fulfil the Law. The slogan of self-sufficiency is an old trick of Satan. Those who believe it, only end up being hypocrites. Paul asserts that the Law is good; but it cannot save man from sin. He says that its role is that of a school master to lead seekers to Christ. He says, 'what the Law was unable to do, God did it in Christ'. Paul declares that the aim of Christ's accomplishment was to see that the righteousness of Law might be fulfilled in those who walk according the Spirit. Why did God send the Spirit of His Son into our hearts? Is it not primarily to enable us to keep His laws? (Eze. 36:27). We cannot fulfil the Law on our own. The role of our faith, after all, is to seek the help of the Spirit in us to walk in His ways.

John says, '… The law was given through Moses; grace and truth came through Jesus Christ.' (Jn. 1:17). Jesus is truth personified. John records, 'Jesus answered, "I am the way and the truth and the life. No one comes to the father except through me"' (Jn. 14:6). Hence salvation is not through Law but through the person Jesus Christ who is full of grace and truth. (Jn. 1:14). His sacrificial death for our sins, His burial and resurrection put together is the Gospel. By this Gospel a man is saved. Paul says that salvation is only through the Gospel. He gives a definition of the Gospel he preached. It is the news that Christ truly died for our sins and rose again on the third day- all according to Scriptures. (I Co. 15:1-4). Paul says, '… We maintain that a man is justified by faith apart from observing the law.' (Ro. 3:28). This is grace!

There are others who talk of grace to undermine the Law. Some in the Church history had gone to the extent of saying that God did away with the Law. They challenge the faithful to cast aside the Law. We are saved by grace through faith – not by works so that no one can boast. All correct. But does it end there? What about good works God prepared in advance for us? Are we not His workmanship created in Christ Jesus to be achievers? (Eph. 2:10). In Jesus truth and grace are in full. His grace is sufficient for all for everything. He enables us to fulfil the Law through faith in Jesus. Jesus declares that he has not come to abolish the Law or the Prophets. He says that even the stroke of a pen in the Law will last until it is accomplished. He cautions against the violation of the Law. (Mt. 5:17-19). Jesus enables us to fulfil the Law. The one who fulfilled can help us to fulfil. Paul uses 'do's and 'don't's from 12ᵗʰ chapter onwards in Romans to teach on Christian everyday life. This may appear like the Law. But it is only 'Christian ethic'. We can infer from his presentation in the book of Romans that God the Father resurrected the Law as 'Christian ethic' when He resurrected His son. The Spirit enables us to have this Christian ethic in our conduct. In Jesus Christ a believer can have truth (the Law) and also grace. These two can be held together- not one in exclusion of the other- to live a fulfilled life.

Individual faith and Corporate faith

Adam was free either to obey God or to disobey. God honours man's freedom. Today man is free either to receive the Gospel or to reject it. A believer in the church is free either to walk according to the Spirit or according to the flesh. Man is free from start to finish. That is why the Gospel is truly personal. We can note this from the following verses: Jesus says, 'Whoever believes and is baptized will be saved, but whoever does not believe will be condemned.' (Mk. 16: 16); Paul and Silas tell the Philippian jailer, 'Believe in the Lord Jesus and you will be saved – you and your household.' (Ac. 16:31); Paul says, '…, "Everyone who calls on the name of the Lord will be saved."' (Ro. 10:13); '… If you confess with your mouth, "Jesus is Lord," and believe in your heart that God raised him from the dead, you will be saved.' (Ro. 10:9).The emphasis here is on a personal commitment. Salvation is personal and individualistic. Christian life also is primarily personal. When Jesus tells His disciples, 'You are the salt of the earth', He has in mind an individual disciple in the society. We know that salt dissolves, but in particles; so does a believer participate individually in the society.

The covenant God made with Abraham includes blessing to all the families of the earth. Rahab's family received the blessing. So did the families of Cornelius, Lydia and the Philippian jailer in New Testament times. Christian faith is shared among members of a family and also a larger group. This faith is called 'corporate faith.' Every member is baptized into the body of Christ. (I Co. 12:13). Individual believers are there in the body. God called you into fellowship with His Son Jesus Christ our Lord. (I Co. 1:9). The Church is a body of 'called out' people. Jesus is the head of the body. God called us to corporate worship. Promise of His presence is also among two or three. Peter makes an elaborate statement about this body corporate describing their role. (I Pe. 2:9). Hence a believer's faith is individual faith and also corporate faith.

A person who puts his trust in Jesus Christ knows how precious his faith is. His faith resulted in salvation. It made him receive the right to be a child of God. He, now, has inheritance in heaven. But there is no place for exclusively individualistic faith life in the Bible. No amount of study of Scripture and prayer can make a believer self-sufficient. Luke in the Acts of the Apostles says that those who accepted Peter's message were baptised and spent time together. (Ac 2:41, 42). We do not see any one individually growing in faith. There is no place for secret faith. The Gospels record that Joseph of Arimathea, a secret believer, had to finally come out in the open after the death of Jesus. (Jn. 19:38).

Then there is the problem of making the 'corporate faith' only 'the faith'. Those who emphasise only corporate faith do it only with an ulterior motive. They are happy if the generations of the former believers continue with them even as nominal Christians. They call it Church centred faith. Pastors may have a tendency to usurp for mediation and to assert their authority. Examples of this in Church history are many. Mediation and authoritarianism have no place in the Church. Paul declares, '... There is one God and one mediator between God and mankind, the man Christ Jesus.' (I Ti. 2:5). God promised to shepherd His sheep personally. 'I myself will tend my sheep and have them lie down, declares the Sovereign LORD.' (Eze. 34:15). Jesus came from the Father and declared Himself as the 'Good Shepherd'. The writer to the Hebrews calls Him the 'Great Shepherd'. The gift of shepherding is given to believers also. It is a valuable gift. It is to be exercised cautiously. Peter identifies himself with his fellow-elders and appeals to them to serve the flock voluntarily as shepherds. He urges them to eagerly serve without greed for money or obsession for power. He asks them to set their eyes on the crown from the 'Chief Shepherd'. (I Pe. 5:1-4). From his exhortation we understand that a pastor is a team leader along with other leaders in the Church without a desire to dominate.

There is need for drawing a line of separation between the seventy, the Lord sent and the presbyters, elders and deacons, Paul and others appointed. The former are privileged to take nothing with them and to stay in houses moving from place to place. (Lk. 10:1-12; Mt. 10:5-15) The Apostles followed them in that line. The Church authorities have, organised groups in set places. (Ac. 14:23). They cannot claim the position of the seventy or that of the Apostles to expect such provision or support in homes. Paul showed in his life the transitory stage between these two categories. He made certain statements to make the Church understand this. (II Co. 11:8, 9).

Then, in regions of mass movements we see competition among the leaders of denominations. It results in demonstrating their specialization for attracting people, more to themselves than to the Lord. Fervour for a Church or a Group or an Organisation instead of fervour for the Lord may lead to Pharisaic fervour. Jesus says, 'Woe to you, teachers of the law and Pharisees, you hypocrites! You travel over land and sea to win a single convert, and when he becomes one, you make him twice as much a son of hell as you are.' (Mt. 23:15).Hence leaders have to be careful. They are to note that 'individual faith' and 'corporate faith' both have to be maintained in a balanced manner.

Quality and Quantity

Quality indicates a degree or level of excellence while quantity indicates an amount or number of things. Here, in the context of Christian ministry, 'quality' is the degree of excellence of a believer or a 'Fellowship' of believers and 'quantity' is the number of believers in a Fellowship. Jesus specifies the characteristics for us to be known as His disciples. It is love for one another. Only this makes people know that we are His disciples. (Jn. 13:34, 35). Christ-likeness is the quality which is required in any Fellowship. (Ac. 4:13) The Fellowship should grow in numbers as well. This is quantity in a Fellowship.

Jesus called His disciples with a purpose. 'He appointed twelve — designating them apostles — that they might be with him and that he might send them out to preach.' (Mk. 3:14). They are to be with Him. It is to a fellowship, He called them. The purpose is to grow from one degree of excellence to another. But what is all this for? It is not for self-contentment or self-aggrandizement. It is for a purpose. It is to send them out to preach. Jesus has a task at hand. It is to bring other sheep which do not belong to this sheep pen. (Jn. 10:16). Jesus takes care of quality in His disciples and asks them to work to bring in others with God's help. That is how He takes care of the quantity. (Mt. 9:37, 38). As co-workers with Jesus, believers too have a job to fulfil. Others should be brought in so that there shall be one flock and one shepherd. So quantity or number to be brought in is also important.

There may be some Fellowships, existing only for themselves as social clubs. This is not God's will. There is so much of imbalance in the way they function. They do not commute between being with Him and going out for Him. They want quality at the cost of quantity. There may be other Fellowships which don't have time for nourishment. There is practically no time for having a share together in spiritual realities. What all that is important for them is numbers. Their spirituality is their ministry and vice versa. They do it all in the name of ministry. Those who emphasise on quality give excuses, quoting God's commandments to the Israelites. They say believers are to live separate from others. But we should not forget that the Israelites are a nation among nations. The Fellowships these days are to be different. We live in a pluralistic society. We cannot afford to be isolated. We need to move into the society. Further, there are some pastors who say their Fellowship is a community of perfected saints. They promote perfectionist tendency in the Fellowship which is unscriptural. John says that we march towards perfection. We become perfect only when Jesus returns or only when we leave this world. In the mean time we long for quality while bringing others to the Fellowship. The Fellowships should hold both quality and quantity in tension.

Plenty and Need

Blessing denotes a bestowal of good usually conceived of as material. 'God blessed Adam and Eve saying, "Be fruitful and increase in number; fill the earth and subdue it. Rule over the fish of the sea and the birds of the air and over every living creature that moves on the ground"' (Ge. 1:28). '... God blessed Noah and his sons the same way. (Ge. 9:1). God promised Abraham with a personal blessing and blessing to all the nations through his posterity. God promised Israelites a land flowing with milk and honey. Moses told the Israelites that the Lord would grant them abundant prosperity. (Dt. 28:11). God promised Solomon riches and honour. (I Ki. 3:13). John in his epistle expressed his desire for Gaius that he might prosper in everything. (III Jn. 1:2). When men were blessed by God they received a state of happiness and well-being.

God's promises of blessing are found in numerous portions of the Scripture. But God's promises of His presence in trouble are also found in the Bible. That is why we find many characters in the Bible who were in a different state from what we understand of a state of blessedness. It puzzles our mind when we think about their circumstances in the light of God's blessing. Job is one such character. This is God's testimony about job to Satan: 'Have you considered my servant Job? There is no one on earth like him; he is blameless and upright, a man who fears God and shuns evil.' (Job 1:8). In spite of this God allows him to go through severe suffering. He lost everything he had. Jesus tells His disciples that they will suffer in His name. He says, 'I have told you these things, so that in me you may have peace. In this world you will have trouble. But take heart! I have overcome the world.' (Jn. 16:33). Paul lists his sufferings in II Corinthians chapter 11. These sufferings also are horrible. How are we to understand this? Paul gives an answer: '... I will boast all the more glad about my weaknesses, so that Christ's power may rest on me. That is why, for Christ's sake, I delight in weaknesses, in insults, in hardships, in persecutions, in difficulties. For when I am weak, then I am strong.' (II Co. 12:9ff, 10).

There is a widespread evangelistic activity in these days. While there are evangelists who are preaching their heart out for the salvation of people, there are some contemporary evangelists who are obsessed with 'prosperity Gospel.' When Gospel itself is the Good News where is the need for preaching promises of God as Good News? Paul pronounces 'anathema' on any one who alters the Gospel including an angel or Paul, he, himself. Prosperity is not always an indication of God's blessing. Paul tells Timothy, 'In fact everyone who wants to live a godly life in Christ will be persecuted.' (II Ti. 3:12). Hence prosperity is only one side of the story. By making it everything preachers make people falter.

On the other hand, there were those who practised poverty as a virtue in Church history. They rigorously practised poverty and voluntarily undertook suffering to grow in faith. There are preachers who challenge believers to practice poverty to earn merit in God's sight these days. This may lead to asceticism. Therefore it is always safe to take everything on our stride as the Lord allows. Paul declares, 'I know what it is to be in need, and I know what it is to have plenty, I have learned the secret of being content in any and every situation, whether well fed or hungry, whether living in plenty or in want.' (Php. 4:12). This is a balanced life of a believer.

Evangelism and Social action

Evangelism is making known the facts of the Gospel. The Gospel is the Good News that God in Jesus Christ has fulfilled His promises to Israel and that a way of salvation is opened to all. The essential message is made more explicit by the death and resurrection of Jesus Christ. Before His ascension, 'He said to them, "Go into all the world and preach the good news to all creation."' (Mk 16:15). Philip, the evangelist had to lead the Ethiopian eunuch, a worshipper of Jehovah, to salvation by explaining to him the Gospel contained in chapter 53 of Isaiah. The Gospel is to be preached for the salvation of men.

World is full of people created by God. He is concerned about their welfare. His concern for the poor is seen in the first five books of the Bible. Solomon talks about the poor at length in proverbs. From the book of Nehemiah we can elicit reasons for poverty. The poor give this information to Nehemiah: Large number of mouths to be fed in the family, indebtedness, loan interest, taxes, oppression etc. are the causes of poverty.(Ne. 5:2-4). This situation continued till the time of Jesus. His mother Mary in the Magnificat exults in joy for what God did for the poor. The characteristics of God and His attitude towards the poor and the downtrodden, presented in Psalm 146, were demonstrated by Jesus in His earthly ministry.

Evangelism gives man an opportunity to begin his faith life. If a man accepts the Gospel, it makes him lead a 'quality' life. Jesus calls this 'eternal life'. It is both physical and spiritual life at one go. He promises to give it abundantly. Then how are the evangelists supposed to respond towards poverty in social life? In the Acts of the Apostles we notice the priority, the Church gave, to helping the poor. Besides recognising the Apostleship of each other, the consensus among the Apostles for the Jews and Apostles for the Gentiles was on helping the poor. Paul says all that the Apostles to the Jews asked them was that he and his associates should continue to remember the poor. He says he too was eager to do this. (Gal. 2:10). Paul calls the generosity of the poor Macedonian

Churches, God's grace given to them. Their contribution for the needy in Jerusalem was commended. (II Co. 8:1, 2).

The Church continued with this vision. Did it lose its vision midway? It appears so. Can it continue without getting back its vision? No. Since the early twentieth century there has been an extra emphasis on social action. The champions of social action go to the extent of defining evangelism as basically social action. Does it hold water? When Mary anointed the feet of Jesus with perfume, Judas Iscariot objected to it. He said it could have been better had the money been given to the poor. But what did Jesus say? He said, "You will always have the poor among you." What did He mean? Caring for the poor is not to be occasional. It is a personal everyday affair. It is more a life style of a believer than an occasional activity. But the death and resurrection of Jesus Christ should be proclaimed. Jesus told His disciples, "As the father has sent me I am sending you." In Jesus we have salvation in all its facets. Even in us evangelism and concern for the poor are not two but they are one. We know that the salvation of the soul is the key factor. Hence the 'Great Commission' is for evangelism which is all-inclusive. Paul says, 'He who did not spare his own Son, but gave him up for us all - how will he not also, along with him, graciously give us all things?' (Ro. 8:32). When a person receives the Gospel, he receives Jesus Christ. In Him he receives all the material blessings as well.

Gifts of the Spirit and Fruit of the Spirit

Spiritual gifts are grace gifts- 'charismata.' These are bestowed on believers for service. Numerous spiritual gifts are mentioned by Paul. (Ro. 12:6-8; I Cor. 12:8-10, 28; Eph. 4:11). The purpose of these gifts is for the common good of the believers. (I Co. 12:4-7). It is to build up the body of Christ, 'the Church'. (I Co. 14:12). Secondarily these gifts are for the conviction and conversion of unbelievers. Paul says that gift of tongues and gift of prophecy are to be exercised in wisdom. He says that when others are present, only the words which they understand are to be uttered. He says these will help them. He concludes saying that such utterance will make them fall down and worship God. (I Co. 14:21-25).

'Fruit of the Spirit' is different from 'Gifts of the Spirit'. 'Fruit of the Spirit' in the Bible is used metaphorically. Paul used it in Galatians,

"… The fruit of the spirit is love, joy, peace, patience, kindness, goodness, faithfulness, gentleness and self-control, Against such things there is no Law.' (Gal. 5:22, 23). 'Fruit of the Spirit' could well be understood as Christian character since a believer is to be conformed into His image. This character shines out in a person's life in its varied expression.

Possessing spiritual gifts is the privilege of God's children. The power of the Holy Spirit is at work in them. Peter reacts in disgust when people glorify them when they healed the crippled man. (Ac. 3:12) The danger of people considering the gift as a person's power is always there. Peter was ruthless in scoring it out. The present day preachers are prone to such temptation. There are many preachers who are making their gift overshadow the Gospel they preach. But a believer should not be obsessed with the desire for displaying spiritual gifts. In this obsession, believers become unmindful of their Christian character which is the fruit of the Spirit. Our being is first and our doing is next. What we are should lead us to what we do. Since the components in the fruit of the Spirit appear simple, believers do not pay attention to these. When the Lord returns, it is into His image we are to be finally transformed. This is fruit of the Spirit in its perfection.

A special mention is needed to be made about healing ministry. There is some teaching promoted to support the healing ministry. They take Isaiah chapter 53 as their basis. They equate healing with forgiveness of sins. They say that since He took upon Him our infirmities, everybody is healed and this healing is to be obtained in faith. Is it true? It makes people feel guilty when they do not receive healing. They think they do not have enough faith. If lack of faith is the reason for absence of healing, why then did the godly suffer in the Bible? Did they not have faith? Why Did Elisha die from illness? (IIKi.13:14).Why does Paul reconcile himself with the reality of a thorn in his flesh? (IICo. 12:8, 9). What about suffering in old age? They say that the Cross took away all sickness. They give equal footing to sin and sickness. We know that Cross takes away punishment of sin that is death. What punishment does it take away of sickness? Is not sickness punishment in itself, if it is taken that way? Further, does not salvation include every physical blessing as well? We can ask God for healing as His children. Believers with a gift of healing can become available to the sick. Further, the sick can call the elders of the Church to pray over them. (Jas. 5:14).No special teaching is necessary. God is patient with those who are culprits. He does not revoke His gifts and His call. (Ro. 11:29).

The fruit of the Spirit is to be coveted. Besides this believers should not be hesitant to recognise and use their gifts. Present day excesses of preachers in exercising spiritual gifts are causing some believers to shy away from using them. Paul exhorts Timothy to fan into flame his spiritual gift. (II Ti. 1:6). The Church is made strong when spiritual gifts are exercised by all. There is no option between 'Gifts of the Spirit' and 'Fruit of the Spirit.' Both are to be coveted. It is in making the Church grow we grow.

Conclusion

Jesus calls the Holy Spirit, 'Spirit of Truth'. He says, 'But when he, the Spirit of Truth, comes, he will guide you into all truth. He will not speak on his own; he will speak only what he hears, and he will tell you what is yet to come.' (Jn. 16:13). The disciples were inspired by the Holy Spirit to write the Epistles, to lead us into all truth. Objective truth when brought into subjective experience leads us to salvation. We admit that God is sovereign while acting responsible. Law and grace both are made available in the person of Jesus who fulfilled the Law. Individual faith and corporate faith keep us safe in the community of God's people. This faith works through love. We long for quality in our Christian life while fervently working for quantity in the Fellowship. We take everything on our stride whether it is plenty or need as the Lord allows. Evangelism and social action keep each one of us as an integrated person commissioned by Jesus into the world. And Gifts of the Spirit and Fruit of the Spirit engage us in the extension of God's kingdom day by day by making us march towards the likeness of His son Jesus Christ. Let us take possession of both the constituents of truth to keep us away from imbalance and faltering.

CHAPTER IV

Experience- Multifarious

Experience is an activity or a practice in doing something. James, the brother of Jesus perhaps put his faith in Jesus only after the death and resurrection of Jesus. He doesn't want either he himself or anyone else waste his time any longer. He wants everyone to be a practical Christian. He says that we deceive ourselves by merely listening the word and not doing. He asks us to do what it says. (Jas. 1:22). After all, response to God's revelation is response to His word. (Eph. 1:13). This is faith in action - the receiving of His promises. It is faith working through love - love, not just in word, but also in deed. This is 'experience' in the life of a believer. Paul says that we have experience of salvation because of our faith in Jesus Christ. (II Tim. 3:15). This experience is the starting point to make us claim all the promises of God. Peter says that God's promises to us are for participation in the divine nature and wants us to be effective and productive in the knowledge of Jesus Christ. (II Pet. 1:4, 8).

The Bible records elaborately various events. These records contain information about persons who in response to the revelation of God act and obtain experience. When we go through such records we are very much impressed by different kinds of their experiences. These differ from one person to another. But all these persons have one thing in common- faith. All of them respond in the same faith. We hear preachers teaching on these Biblical characters. There is a possibility for these teachers to ignore teaching about the faith of the Biblical characters. Instead there can be elaborate teaching on their experience. False teaching may take the form of challenging believers to long, exclusively, for the only one experience of one particular character in the Bible. When believers respond to such challenges, they tend to act in a way which may not suit their situation or their need. Such Christian experience remains superficial. Sharing of that experience with others may bring about shallow faith in their Fellowship. This experience may become prototype in that Fellowship. Believers divided on the lines of experience cannot show unity of faith which the word of God demands. You have before you different characters in the Bible with different kinds of experiences. You have just begun to claim the promises of God. You can choose to claim any of the promises of God according to your situation and need.

Finding God's will

"Whoever does God's will is my brother and sister and mother." (Mk. 3:35).

In the recent years there is much talk on finding God's will. Those who talk about God's will keep the experience of some Biblical characters in that area as their basis. It is wonderful to know God's will and it is much more wonderful to try doing it and doing it! Besides this, finding God's will becomes necessary in a person's life at one time or another. We reach cross roads in our life and look for some guidance not knowing which way to turn. The best way in such circumstances is to find a character in the Bible who went through such experience. Is there an example in the Bible of someone seeking God's will and doing it?

Eleazar is a good example. He looked for God's will with regard to the marriage of the son of his master Abraham. He found it and executed it. There are others who have that experience. Gideon found out that he was called and then he proceeded. David found out the will of God before going for a battle and went and won the battle. Joseph was led by the Angel in dreams in marrying Mary and then protecting the baby Jesus. In the garden of Gethsemane, Jesus voluntarily submitted Himself to the will of the Father. Paul received guidance and went to Macedonia.

Eleazar found out God's will and carried it out. He chose one method for finding God's will. He told God that he would ask for water and would consider that girl as God's choice, who would offer water not only to him but also to his camels. (Ge. 24:43, 44). Gideon found out from God whether He would save Israel, by another method. It is by placing a wool fleece on the threshing floor and asking God to deal with it. (Jdg. 6:36-40). David found out the will of God by using ephod. (I Sa. 30:7, 8). Joseph was led by an Angel in a dream. (Mt. 2:13). Jesus directly conversed with His Father and obeyed His will. (Mt. 26:39). The disciples chose Matthias in the place of Judas by lots. (Ac. 1:26). Paul was led by a vision. (Ac. 16:9).

We notice from the Bible that there are various ways in which men of God found God's will. Jesus said that he had come to this earth to do the will of His Father. He revealed His mind concerning His relationship with people. He said that only those who do God's will are related to him as brother, sister and mother. (Mk. 3:34, 35). It is no wonder that every one of us would love to do God's will to claim such relationship.

There was one specific time in my life, when I had to look for God's will. I was working as a lecturer, at Noble College, Machilipatnam, India, which is a secular college founded in 1843 by the Church Missionary Society. In 1994, on May 7, the Principal sent a word to me saying that I should go to Germany on an exchange programme. I thought for a few days about the assignment and then told my wife and children that I had decided not to go. I told them that climate in Germany would not suit me. My elder son was irritated at this and said, "You always talk about God's will. Why don't you trust that it is God's will?" I was annoyed at his question and went into the room, closed the door and prayed for God's will in this matter. I turned to my daily readings. That was from the 'Good Seed' of May 9. In this, an old believing woman, tells the leader of the group that he should not say that climate in Canada will not suit them for settlement as refugees in response to his statement. She exhorts him about the protection of God. It came straight to me. I was able to sense that the Lord was speaking to me saying that I should not be afraid of the climate in Germany. Later our Bishop, the chairman of the college said, 'as Paul went on missionary journey we want you to go.' The following Sunday while entering the Church, hesitant still to obey God's will, I asked God to confirm His will through the pastor who had already begun preaching. As I sat in the pew, the pastor said, 'You don't have a purpose and you don't have a goal but God has a plan for you; you obey His word'.

I surrendered to His will and went to Germany. While attending my college duties in Germany, I started making friendship with the students in that college. I spent time in sharing the Gospel in my conversation with each one. I was enjoying personal evangelism. Days went by and exactly at the time of my departure from Germany, one student who was just returning from a holiday met me. I had shared the Gospel with him earlier. He bid me good bye saying, 'Paul I believe God sent you'. I was pleasantly surprised; I was strangely moved; I boarded the plane and came back to India; I returned home stronger physically, mentally and spiritually. I believe God gave me this experience to show me how thrilling it would be to find out God's will and to do it.

There are many books written on 'Finding God's Will.' There are many who teach on this subject at length. They challenge the new believers to live a true spiritual life by finding God's will. Those who try to rise to their challenges tend to believe that it is the only way to please God. They tend to become methodical and they lose spontaneity in their spiritual life. Their dependence on the Holy Spirit for continuous living is hindered by occasional fervour.

This is my question now: Does not God's word reveal God's will? According to Jesus 'doers of God's will' (Mk. 3:35) are those who hear God's word and put it into practice. (Lk. 8:21). Much of God's will is revealed to us in God's word both by specific utterance and example. The following are some of the verses connected with the revealed will of God: Jesus says that it is not the will of God that anyone should be lost. (Mt. 18:14); He declares that it is the Father's will that everyone who looks to the Son and believes in Him shall have eternal life. (Jn.

6:39, 40); Paul says that it is God's will for each one to be sanctified keeping away sexual immorality. (I Th. 4:3); According to him giving thanks in all circumstances is God's will. (I Th. 5:18); He says that it is God's will that each one is to be filled with the Spirit instead of with wine and that singing, rejoicing and being thankful is the will of God for everyone. (Eph. 5:17-20). God's will is clearly revealed in the Bible.

Do we have the right to look for the will of God on a specific matter when we do not care for the revealed will of God? The following are the exhortations given to the believers to receive the ability for doing His will: God says, 'I will instruct you and teach you in the way you should go; I will counsel you and watch over you. Do not be like the horse or the mule, which have no understanding but must be controlled by bit and bridle or they will not come to you.' (Ps. 32:8, 9); Paul urges, 'Do not conform any longer to the pattern of this world, but be transformed by the renewing of your mind. Then you will be able to test and approve what God's will is — his good, pleasing and perfect will.' (Ro. 12:2). From Paul's approach we understand that God's will is not the starting point. There is a process which begins by offering ourselves as a living sacrifice. Then, the renewing of our mind takes place by reading God's word regularly and obeying it. After this we resist the world and abstain from being conformed to its pattern. Then we will be able to test and approve what God's will is- His good, pleasing and perfect will. There is also a concept called 'God's general will.' We can take it as a light for our path before we take a step forward with the lamp we have. (Ps. 119: 105). Further, God's word says that we can trust and rest. Why struggle to find God's will on a matter when another way is also acceptable to God?

Committing our ways to God

"In all your ways acknowledge Him and He will make your paths straight." (Pr. 3:6).

To commit is to entrust for safe keeping. God is worthy of trust. His faithfulness is seen everywhere in the Bible. He is covenant keeping God. He is the one who called us to the fellowship of His son. He is able to keep us from falling. His fatherly care is available to every believer. It is always safe to commit our ways to God. There are quite a few preachers who exhort us to commit our ways to God. There comes a time in our life when we give up all our faith in our wisdom and abandon our ways to God. It is greatly satisfying to see the outcome as the straightened path by God. Is there an example in the Bible of someone committing her ways to God and seeing the outcome as God's doing?

Ruth is a good example. Her father-in-law died. Later her brother-in-law and her husband also died. During this period perhaps she was led to faith in Jehovah by her mother-in-law. Naomi set out on journey back to Israel from Moab. She pleaded with her Moabitish daughters-in-law to stay back in their land and remarry. The elder agreed and stayed back. But Ruth said, 'Don't urge me to leave you or to turn back from you. Where you go I will go and where you stay I will stay. Your people will be my people and your God my God. Where you die I will die and there I will be buried. May the lord deal with me, be it ever so severely, if anything but death separates you and me.' (Ru 1:16, 17). We notice that Ruth did not know what the outcome would be. She committed her way to the Lord in whom her mother-in-law believed. We know what an amount of blessing she received. Boaz married her. And Jesus was born in his lineage. Matthew records the name of Ruth in the genealogy of Jesus.

The Lord says, 'Be still and know that I am God; I will be exalted among the nations, I will be exalted in the earth.' (Ps. 46:10). God says that our salvation is in repentance and trust and that is our strength. (Isa. 30:15). David says that the battle is the Lord's when he goes against Goliath. (I Sa. 17:47). Jehoshaphat learns from the Lord that the battle is not his, but God's. (II Ch. 20:15)

My wife Suguna has this experience of committing her ways to God. She and I had been in courtship before we got married. Her father, Dr. Tekumalla Rama Rao, a Brahmin, was the Principal of 'The Narsapur College', where we studied. On her request, her classmate, a believer, gave her two books - one written by Dr.Billy Graham and another by Saint Sadhu Sundar Singh. Once, during this time, I asked her to attend the Gospel meetings of Dr.Akbar Haqq who was an associate of Dr. Billy Graham, at Narsapur. She attended one meeting and committed her life to Christ. Incidentally, I too committed my life to Christ on one of the following meetings. Her parents put her away from college not only because she confessed Jesus as her Lord but also because she said that she would marry me. They had confined her to the house for nearly four years. During this time she was cut away from all possibilities of meeting Christians and attending Church. She made use of the Bible her father had in his library. She used to read the book of Psalms. She made up her mind to commit her problem of marriage to God. She committed her ways to the omniscient God. He straightened her path. Her marriage with me took place soon. God gave her this experience to prove that He is the caring father. There is none who put his trust in Him and is let down.

But there might be some occasions when God wants us to act. When He reveals His faithfulness, He expects us to act in response to it. He enables us to collect His provision only when we take a step of faith. Moses saw the power of God in delivering the Israelites from the Egyptian bondage. When they were caught between the Red sea and the Egyptian army, Moses encouraged them saying that the Lord would fight for them. But it appears that something more was needed from Moses. That was 'an action in faith.' God saw that it was wanting in Moses. Instead of crying out to God he was to ask the Israelites to move on. (Ex. 14:15). Joshua lamented over the defeat of the Israelites by their enemies. What needed at the time was not trust and prayer but an action on the one who sinned. (Jos. 7:10, 11). Prayers of commitment have their own value. Exhortations in this regard sound very spiritual. But these are the questions which need answers: Does God expect us to commit our ways to Him in all situations in our life ignoring lethargy and inaction on our part? Why is there so much of exhortation in the Bible for Christian action in freedom? Where is the guarantee that absence of Christian courage does not take shelter in the so called 'committing our ways to Him'? Further, besides committing our ways, there is the possibility of living with an attitude of love towards God. Supposing we continue to love Him irrespective of our persistent difficulties, does God leave us? No. He does not. He keeps working for us.

Loving God

"And we know that in all things God works for the good of those who love Him, who have been called according to His purpose." (Ro. 8:28).

Love is God's benevolence towards mankind. When applied to man it is an affectionate devotion towards God. The book of Hosea contains the strained love relationship between God and Israel. God is so very concerned about the love of His people. (Hos. 2:23). Once a man is born again, he is constantly exhorted to love God. John speaks much about love in his epistles. From his epistles we understand that loving God is an act only in response to the love we receive from God. (I Jn. 4:10, 19). Paul says that God has poured out His love into our hearts by the Holy Spirit. (Ro. 5:5). It is wonderful to be lost in His love irrespective of situations only to become conscious at the end that God wrought those for our good. And it was all for our transformation into His likeness. Is there an example in the Bible of a man who loved God in all situations only to know at the end that everything that had happened, happened for his good?

Joseph is a good example. We understand that he was brought up in close communion with his God. He saw in his childhood, visions from God not knowing what the visions really meant. His elder brothers grew jealous of him. Joseph was sold to the Ishamaelites. He was taken to Egypt. Pothiphar one of Pharaoh's officials bought him. In all these situations he never blamed God. And the Lord was with him. For a brief time he lived in peace. But he was thrown into prison when Pothiphar's wife tricked him after being refused by him to cooperate with her in sex. The Lord was with him there as well. He was lifted up when he told the king the meaning of his dream through revelation from God. He became the Prime Minister of Egypt. Later his brothers had to go over to Egypt to buy grain for their survival. Joseph subsequently revealed to them his identity and he provided his father and all the members of the family with everything in Egypt. Later his father died. After his death, Joseph's brothers were afraid that he would harm them. So they tried to convey to him that their father had requested Joseph to forgive them. Joseph was terribly upset. He wanted them to have an overall view of all that had happened. He said, 'You intended to harm me but God intended it for good to accomplish what is now being done, the saving of many lives.' (Ge. 50:20). Joseph saw in his life how God worked everything for his good.

Some members of our Church in Machilipatnam used to go for outreach to the nearby villages. An elder of our Church introduced me to the congregations in different villages. I developed great liking for the people in those villages. Seeing this he asked me to be responsible for a small congregation formed in a village. In my enthusiasm and love for the Lord I began working very hard. In spite of my regular visits, for a number of years, the congregation had a very slow and insignificant growth. This used to be of much concern to me. I identified myself totally with the congregation. I was sharing in their joys and sorrows. One of them was a recently baptized young widow with two daughters. She had been a heart patient. She became sick and was admitted in the hospital. Her mother, who had all along been avoiding the Gospel, was attending on her at the hospital. I visited the widow almost every day and fasted and prayed for her recovery many times. During this time the congregation was waiting for a miracle while other villagers were waiting curiously. She died in the hospital after 40 days.

The village elders turned down our claim for Christian burial to her. I was greatly shocked and the small congregation was thoroughly shaken. In a dramatic turn and to the astonishment of the villagers, the mother and brother of the widow put their faith in Jesus. We all praised God. After the death of the widow, her friend got upset and an evil-spirit took possession of her. There was a great turmoil in the village. The villagers were very much afraid. I was asked to go there and help her. I took three of my younger fellow believers along with me. The evil-spirit left her when four of us prayed for her. The villagers were awe struck when they saw that the evil-spirit was driven out. The Church in that village came back stronger than it was, exactly at a time when everybody in the village was expecting that the congregation would leave the Church. In the following year the Church increased three fold in its number. I realized for sure that all things work together for good to them that love God and are called according to His purpose.

We may be good at loving God. What about loving our fellow man? What does God want? The Israelites claim the covenant of God with

Abraham for themselves. In so doing they ignore the latter part of the covenant. God promised Abraham saying that through his offspring all the nations of the earth will be blessed. (Ge. 22:18). They look down upon the rest of the mankind. From Paul's writings we notice that Gentiles were called uncircumcised, separate from Christ, excluded from citizenship in Israel, foreigners to the covenant and without hope and without God in the world. (Eph. 2:11, 12). Paul says that God's promise of blessing is for all others also. (Eph. 2:13). The blessing for the Israelites was intended to flow to others. God's love which is shed abroad in our hearts is intended to flow to others.

Jesus sums up the commandments of God into two. "'The most important one," answered Jesus, "is this: 'Hear, O Israel, the Lord our God, the Lord is one. Love the Lord your God with all your heart and with all your soul and with all your mind and with all your strength.' The second is this: 'Love your neighbour as yourself.' There is no commandment greater than these."' (Mk 12:29-31). The second one is often ignored. John in his epistles comes heavily on those who are guilty of not showing love for both God and the fellow man. Following is his comment: 'If anyone says, "I love God," yet hates his brother, he is a liar. For anyone who does not love his brother, whom he has seen, cannot love God, whom he has not seen.' (I Jn. 4:20). So the promise of 'God working all things for our good' is a conditional promise. It can be received by those who love God in the true sense of the word.

Teachers often emphasise on loving God invariably with a promise of receiving good from Him. They project it as a bargain. Further, they might not sometimes distinguish between punishment and trial when believers suffer. Believers may suffer when God punishes. 'Loving God' may be presented to them as a solution for coming out of punishment. They may not talk of repentance. God hates love from an unrepentant heart. Further, when Paul talks of 'all things working together for good', he has primarily the spiritual progress of the believer in his mind. (Ro. 8:28-30). Do we long for the likeness of His Son in us? As teachers, do we make the believers give greater importance to spiritual blessing than to material blessing? If a believer gives greater importance to spiritual blessing it is because of his renewed mind. He is not wrong if he specifically chooses what is good for him and asks Him to grant it.

Asking God

"If you remain in me and my words remain in you, ask whatever you wish, and it will be given you." (Jn. 15:7).

'To ask' here, means to seek to obtain from God. Jesus says, 'Ask and it will be given to you.' God gives because of His benevolence towards mankind. The present day evangelistic movement is geared towards the experience of asking God and receiving from Him. Some itinerant evangelists encourage people to believe in Jesus so that they can ask Him for their needs. It is a great challenge in pluralistic society when Jesus is presented as a prayer answering God. People respond to such challenges and tell God that they would believe if their need is met. It is amazing to hear many testimonies from them about God's response to their prayers. There is an example in the Bible of a woman in need who had asked God specifically for something and obtained from Him.

Hannah is a good example. Hannah, the first wife of Elkanah, had been childless. His second wife who had children kept provoking Hannah till she wept and would not eat. It appears she had been waiting for children primarily to overcome this situation. Suddenly wisdom dawned on her. She prayed to God for a son promising that she would give him to the Lord and would abstain from using a razor on his head. Trusting in God's promise she rested. After this her face was never downcast. God answered her prayer. A son was born to her. She stood by her vow. The child was given over to God. And that is Samuel, the first of the prophetic order.

My wife has some experience of this kind. She had remained a housewife till our children grew up. Then she applied for a Government paid teaching job. The employment opportunities being scarce and her age nearing the upper limit, she was aware of what meagre chances she stood. She opted to specifically pray to God to give her that job. Matters appeared impossible to move in her favour. The permission of the Government was needed to fill the post. While approaching the authorities in the Government she kept the story of the widow and the unjust judge on her mind. She repeatedly sought the able hand of the Lord and the Lord made the authorities show mercy on her. Procedural difficulties cleared away by themselves. For reasons best known to them, the school authorities decided to fill a higher post than the one advertised. It was to our great amazement that she was appointed in that higher post.

Asking God and receiving from His hand is a wonderful experience. But in these days asking God and persevering with the request is considered by some as spiritual maturity. In other words answering our prayers is considered God's privilege. There is a feeling promoted that we are doing a favour to God by our asking Him. Preachers give an impression that it is godliness. What a travesty of truth! Besides this, the primary object for asking is also ignored. Jesus has in His mind the greatest of the gifts, the Holy Spirit, when He exhorted them to ask. (Lk. 11:9-13).

Further, God's promises to God's children are conditional. '"Because he loves me," says the LORD, "I will rescue him; I will protect him, for he acknowledges my name. He will call upon me, and I will answer him; I will be with him in trouble, I will deliver him and honour him. With long life will I satisfy him and show him my salvation"' (Ps. 91:14-16). Jesus lays down some conditions while exhorting His disciples to ask. (Jn. 15:7). Abiding in Him is not an occasional act. A branch remains in the vine, to bear fruit. A believer should remain in Jesus to bear fruit. God's word should flow in him as sap flows in a branch. Receiving God's word is not to be with intervals. Besides this, what does it mean to ask in His name? What does His name stand for? Jesus taught us to pray to the Father saying 'hallowed be your name.' We should not misuse it. God commands saying, 'You shall not misuse the name of the LORD your God, for the LORD will not hold anyone guiltless who misuses his name.' (Ex. 20:7). Asking in itself is no virtue. If they ask for the sake of asking, believers are bound to be frustrated. Further, we may put God to test while asking for something. Jesus refused to ask for the protection of angels when the devil suggested it to Him. (Mt. 4:7). God sees our motive when we go to Him in prayer. James points out that when we ask, we do not receive, because we ask with wrong motives- that we may spend what we get on our pleasures. (Jas. 4:3, 4). Besides all these, does He not know our need? Does He not provide for us as our caring Father? Jesus says, '... The pagans run after all these things, and your heavenly Father knows that you need them.' (Matt. 6:32).

Seeking God's kingdom

"But seek first His kingdom and his righteousness and all these things will be given to you as well." (Mt. 6:33).

'To seek', here, means to try to obtain. Kingdom of God is the Christ centred rule of God. Paul says God made Jesus the centre of everything. He says, '...Through him to reconcile to himself all things, whether things on earth or things in heaven, by making peace through his blood, shed on the cross.' (Col. 1:20). Jesus exhorts His disciples to seek the kingdom of His Father and His moral character and leave their anxieties in the world to Him. A Christian lives in two worlds at the same time. He is placed by God in this world and at the same time he is seated in the heavenly places. He is constantly exhorted to live a life of a sojourner as his true citizenship is in heaven. Yet he is asked to be salt and light to this earth. He has to meet his own needs when he continues to live on this earth. But he is not supposed to be anxious about these. His mind is to be set on God's kingdom and His righteousness. These are to be his first priority. Then the caring Father looks after all his needs. Is there a character in the Bible who lived his life as a real sojourner?

Abraham is a typical example of a sojourner. God called him to leave his country, his people and his father's household and go to the land that He would show. He promised that He would bless him. Abraham believed God and went. He always set his mind on God's kingdom and His righteousness. Once four kings seized all the goods of Sodom and Gomorrah and carried off those along with Lot, his women and his people. When Abraham came to know about this, he chased them with his trained men and routed the enemy and brought back Lot, his women, people and possessions. The king of Sodom was very much pleased with this and asked Abraham to keep back the possessions. Abraham said that he had taken an oath that he would accept nothing belonging to him, not even the thread or the thong of a sandal so that he would never be able to say that he made Abraham rich. (Ge. 14:23). He lived in tents. But he never lacked anything. God took care of all his needs and Abraham had everything in abundance. 'Abram had become very wealthy in livestock and in silver and gold.' (Ge. 13:2).

In my childhood days I used to dream of possessing a house in the manner described in my English language lesson 'Ideal House.' But after I committed my life to Christ those thoughts left me. My wife and I were, always, spending time in attending believers' retreats and camps for learning and preaching. Years were rolling by. I did not even buy a piece of land to build a house. When the authorities of our Church were selling the vacant land in plots, I was refused to even apply as they had a stipulation in membership rules which I did not satisfy that time. All those who were allotted paid in part. Later there was a court case against the authorities. After a long time it got cleared. When they made the layout again they found some extra plots. They sent word to me asking me to pay some money as advance and receive the allotment letter. My brother advanced that money. I received the allotment letter. I repaid the money back shortly to my brother and paid the rest at the time of registration from the unexpected arrears of pay I received from the government. Later God granted me 'my childhood desire' of an ideal house by providing me with an opportunity to stay for six years in the only quarters our college has. It is like a farm house with a pond where I reared various kinds of birds and fish. I saw His hand not only in all this but also in the subsequent provision of rather a comfortable house, with many fruit bearing trees and flower plants. (Dt. 6:10,11).

Jesus says that God will give all those things that He mentioned, as well, if you seek God's kingdom and his righteousness in the first place. This statement may arouse many doubts. The following are some of these: Did not God tell Adam that he would eat his food by the sweat of his brow? ; What about Psalm 128 where in, a promise is found about enjoying the fruit of one's hands? ; Solomon says that there is nothing better for a man than to enjoy his work, because that is his lot. (Ecc. 3:22); Jesus in his parables talks of hard work and commends it. Is ambition wrong? ; Does not a definite effort to provide for oneself and for his household find a scriptural sanction? ; Paul finds fault with those who do not provide for his family and for his relatives. (I Ti. 5:8); Paul demands hard work from the believers; He asks those who are stealing to stop it and work with their own hands to provide for those who are in need. (Eph. 4:28); He commands idle people to earn the bread they eat. (II Th. 3:10-12). So what Jesus was saying in the 'Sermon on the Mount' was not that His followers should leave their daily labour but that they should relinquish all anxiety about tomorrow. He asked them to pray for their daily bread so that they would live one day at a time; For, God provided Israelites, manna, one day at a time. Further, He was exhorting them to set their priorities right. Their scale of preference was to be recast. Their value system was to be adjusted. The key factor in their life should be the extension of God's kingdom established in God's righteousness. As believers we should examine our life style to know whether the qualities of the kingdom community are present in us or not. God's righteousness is made available to us as right relationship with God and right living in the world. Jesus concludes His 'Sermon on the Mount' by asking the community to seek for such life of purposefulness- the life built on a rock.

Conclusion

The Bible contains different kinds of human experiences. Each person received from God according to his or her need, in faith. Only a few of these are listed above. Our questions under each type of experience remain unanswered if we seek one experience in exclusion of all others. Instead, if we keep ourselves open to receive His favour, He will lead us through various kinds of experiences in different situations arising in our life: God's will should be found when needed and it should be done; We should commit all our ways to Him and He will straighten our path; We should abide in Him and let His word abide in us. Then we can ask in His name and obtain our needs; we should love God in all situations and God will see that all things work together for our good and we should seek His kingdom and His righteousness and He will provide all our needs. These exhortations are not to be considered as one elbowing all others out. All these exhortations are in fact 'the will of God' revealed in the Scripture. These, when received will enrich the experience of a believer in this world. We will become impoverished if one experience is chosen in exclusion of all other kinds. Let us be rich in His grace by keeping ourselves open to all these.

CHAPTER V

Grace- Multi channelled

G od's children have 24 hours in a day as all others have. The time of God's children is to be employed purposefully. We need to physically engage ourselves in various fields of activity. Since God doesn't need to operate in vacuum, our daily activities which He purposed, serve Him as a means for imparting His Grace to us. In the Old Testament all objects, all gatherings and all festivals had a purpose. In all these, the common feature was God's presence and His blessing upon the Israelites. God the creator is also the one who sustains His creation. He Himself gives all men life and breath and everything. (Ac. 17:25). He revealed Himself in time and space situations to man so that he might find Him. Now He commands all people everywhere to repent. Those who repent and accept the Gospel receive His gift of salvation. They are in Christ and they become His new creation. (II Co. 5:17).

Paul tells the Ephesian believers that they are saved by God's grace. His grace which is sufficient for salvation is sufficient for sustaining a believer. Paul talks about his hard work and attributes it to the grace which is available for continuing in His service. (I Co. 15:10). Sustaining grace is through the Spirit He put in a believer's heart. He says that God has made us competent as ministers of a new covenant. (II Co. 3:6). According to Paul there is no reason for boasting as what we have is only what we have received. (I Co. 4:7). He declares, 'Now it is God who makes us stand firm in Christ. (II Co. 1:21). Paul claims with assurance, 'I can do everything through him who gives me strength.' (Php. 4:13). So it is grace from start to finish in the faith life of a believer. The Holy Spirit dispenses God's grace through various means. False teaching may take the form of confining believers to only one means of grace. This is an error of proportions. It is God's desire that you should be nourished well so that you grow from strength to strength to be able to work in His vineyard.

In one student meeting, I spoke about the terribleness of fleshly desires and the need for overcoming these. I gave an instant solution to overcome the flesh. I concluded saying, 'walk in the Spirit and you will not fulfil your fleshly desires.' When I was about to leave the hall, a student came to me with sincere expectation and asked me to tell him what it all meant to walk in the Spirit. I had no answer. I went home; I went through an intense struggle and looked from God for the meaning of 'walking in the spirit'. My eyes fell on some portions of Scripture which are connected with the activity of the Holy Spirit. The following are the key verses in those portions. They relate to various means through which grace is channelled.

God's word

"For prophecy never had its origin in the will of man, but men spoke from God as they were carried along by the Holy Spirit." (II. Pe. 1:21).

The scripture is of divine origin. It is of God, spoken by men. But one who inspired them to speak was the Holy Spirit. Walking in the Spirit has much to do with the Scriptures. Scripture is given to us as God's truth objectively. It is to be received with reverence. Then it comes into our subjective experience. Scripture is the greatest means through which God supplies His strength. Jesus said, 'It is written: "Man does not live on bread alone, but on every word that comes from of the mouth of God"' (Mt. 4:4). Those who look for walking according to the Spirit would receive God's word-daily: in the morning, at midday and in the night; weekly: at Sunday Worship and in the midweek Bible Study; round the year: on radio, T.V. and in the special meetings; personally: during quiet time.

The Bible contains history, philosophy, science, Poetry etc. But the aim of Scripture is not to present Bible as a book of any one of these. The aim is to lead man to the experience of salvation through faith in Jesus Christ and to lead man to live a down to earth, everyday practical life. It is life in abundance. It is eternal life - a blending of physical and spiritual. The wisdom literature of Solomon is for everyday living. The prologue of Proverbs gives the purpose. It goes like this: 'The proverbs of Solomon son of David, king of Israel: for attaining wisdom and discipline; for understanding words of insight; for acquiring a disciplined and prudent life, doing what is right and just and fair; for giving prudence to the simple, knowledge and discretion to the young - let the wise listen and add to their learning, and let the discerning get guidance- for understanding proverbs and parables, the sayings and riddles of the wise. The fear of the LORD is the beginning of knowledge, but fools despise wisdom and discipline.' (Pr.1:1-7). 'Ecclesiastes' presents the vanity of life in the absence of a purpose. The unique research of Solomon on human life was to present the purpose of human existence. Solomon presents his thesis in Ecclesiastes. He draws us to his conclusion. He says that our existence has a purpose. It is to fear God and keep His Commandments. (Ecc. 12:13, 14). Solomon's 'Song of Songs' presents, the greatest of those which remain in human experience. It is love. It presents love between a man and a woman as ordained by God. It is delight to the eyes. Friends say, 'we rejoice and delight in you we will praise your love more than wine.' Friends are amazed at this love. They say, 'Who is this coming up from the desert leaning on her lover?'

God's word also keeps us away from sin in all areas of life. The Psalmist tells God, 'I have hidden your word in my heart that I might not sin against you.' (Ps. 119:11). 'Your word is a lamp to my feet and a light for my path.' (Ps. 119:105). If we take one step forward, confessing and forsaking sin, the lamp moves forward as a torch light and shows light for a second step. The general illumination becomes any way available for our way. God's word is also for our multifarious needs. Different portions of the Scripture or different applications of the same Scripture come to our help in different everyday situations. But obsession with select portions of the Scripture, favourite preachers, set times for study and chosen themes and characters, restrict our receiving of His word.

There are other hindrances. Philosophy is basically the love of knowledge. There are those who study the Bible to acquire knowledge. In their pursuit of knowledge they do not hesitate to super impose any system of religious thought on Biblical thought. These thoughts might have been framed by learned men according to the elementary principles of the world. Those who acquire such knowledge besides Biblical knowledge may be considered Bible scholars. The person and work of Christ is not central in their system of thought. They lead believers astray by their vain philosophy. These days it has become fashionable to preach general topics in Churches. General topics are needed but they are to be dealt in the light of the Bible. Some preachers do not quote from it. Even when they quote, they quote only in support of what they want to say. They take it for granted that everyone in the congregation knew the Bible. It is not true. Even if it is true, it is no excuse. Preachers who want to preach God's word always preach from the Bible. They employ every other thing, only to make it serve as a vehicle to communicate God's word.

There are others who emphasise, only, reading of the Scripture at the expense of all other means of grace. What about prayer? During Nehemaiah's time they gave equal time for reading of Scripture and for prayer. He records, 'They stood where they were and read from the Book of the Law of the LORD their God for a quarter of the day, and spent another quarter in confession and in worshiping the LORD their God.' (Ne. 9:3). Prayer is another means of grace which is equally important.

Prayer

"In the same way, the Spirit helps us in our weakness. We do not know what we ought to pray for, but the Spirit himself intercedes for us with groans that words cannot express." (Ro. 8:26).

The Holy Spirit is behind prayer. Prayer is speaking to God. It can take the form of praise, thanksgiving, prayer, supplication or even conversation. The Holy Spirit who is the 'paraclete' of the believer comes to his help in communicating with the Father when he does not know how to pray appropriately. (Ro. 8:26). David's praise and worship in Psalms, Hezekiah's thanksgiving in Isaiah chapter 38, Jehoshaphat's prayer in II Chronicles chapter 20, Solomon's supplication in I Kings chapter 8 and Nehemaiah's conversation in the book of Nehemaiah are recorded in the Bible. In communication with God, conversation as a way, is all the more important, as we belong to Him all the time. Nehemaiah is both a man of prayer and a man of action. He converses with God while working. Here are a few of his conversations with God: 'Hear us, O our God, for we are despised. Turn their insults back on their own heads. Give them over as plunder in a land of captivity. Do not cover up their guilt or blot out their sins from your sight, for they have thrown insults in the face of the builders.' (Ne. 4:4, 5); 'Remember me with favour, O my God, for all I have done for these people.' (Ne. 5:19); 'They were all trying to frighten us, thinking, "Their hands will get too weak for the work, and it will not be completed." But I prayed, "Now strengthen my hands."' 'Remember Tobiah and Sanballat, O my God, because of what they have done; remember also the prophetess Noadiah and the rest of the prophets who have been trying to intimidate me.' (Ne. 6:9, 14); 'Remember me for this, O my God, and do not blot out what I have so faithfully done for the house of my God and its services.' (Ne. 13:14).

Praise and worship, thanksgiving, prayer, supplication and conversation are the ways of communication with God. Our Lord's 'High Priestly' prayer in John chapter 17 is an all-in-one communication with the Father. There is every possibility for imbalance in the prayer life of a believer, if teachers emphasise on only one form of communication-usually prayer for his personal needs. So depending on the situation, we should be willing to have times of worship, praise and thanksgiving, prayer, supplication and conversation.

Jesus taught His disciples how to pray in the Sermon on the Mount. 'The Lord's Prayer' shows how the disciples should be concerned about God's kingdom on one hand and about their earthly life on the other.

When they pray they are to pray as Jesus taught them to pray. There are some who do not allow their congregation to repeat the Lord's Prayer. They say it is given only as a pattern. This is partly true. Jesus gave this prayer not only as a pattern but also as the very prayer they are to say when they meet. Luke also records the words of Jesus. Here Jesus says 'when you pray' and then teaches the prayer. (Lk. 11:2-4). From this we understand that it is a prayer to be said as well. Further, this is the only prayer given, to pray as a community of God's children. Let us not allow them to deprive us of the privilege of corporate prayer. It is a prayer when two or three are gathered together in His name.

Jesus taught at length about prayer in the Sermon on the Mount. How often we tend to pray in the manner of people around us, vainly as others and also to show off as the Pharisees. Those prayers do not cause others join with us and the power of two or three gathering together in His name is not availed. Further, God's children can call Him, 'Abba, father.' It is an intimate expression possible only to his children who have the Spirit of His Son in them. (Gal. 4:6). Prayers to the Father without the Spirit of the Son tend to be hypocritical. The Holy Spirit would be there to help if only we had learnt to lean on the Spirit. We should pray to the Father in the name of Jesus and in the Holy Spirit.

Prayer is supernatural communication between man and God. Mystics in Eastern religions claim this communication. They claim to have obtained union with God by spiritual contemplation and self-surrender. In our enthusiasm to have close communication with God we tend to welcome mystic influences. The self-surrender of mystics involves basically emptying of the mind. But a Christian mind is to be full of His word. We pray in complete alertness of mind.

There are some teachers who attribute merit to our prayers. They often quote the instance of Jacob wrestling with God. The Scripture says that he pleaded with God in tears. (Hos. 12:4). Let us not forget the fact that prayer is only a means but not a merit to receive God's favour. Besides this there are conditions to be fulfilled to receive answers from God. We need to abide in Him and let His word abide in us. When teachers over emphasise the importance of prayer, they give the impression that prayer is everything in Christian faith. Do they not recognise other means of grace?

Baptism

"For we were all baptized by one Spirit into one body-whether Jews or Greeks, slave or free-and we were all given the one Spirit to drink." (I Co. 12:13).

Baptism is the work of the Holy Spirit. Baptism is an outward expression of the inward experience. The Ethiopian eunuch; the finance officer; Cornelius, the centurion; Lydia, the business woman and Philippian Jailer and scores of others took baptism soon after they believed. All these New Testament baptisms fit into the meaning of the word 'baptizo', which indicates immersion. All those who were baptized were adults. Their baptism was 'adult baptism'. When Jesus was baptized, the Spirit of God descended on Him like a dove. The Father testified of the Son, expressing His delight. (Mt. 3:16, 17). Baptism is a God given sacrament. It gives an opportunity to a person to identify himself with the community of God's children. It helps him to break away from the wicked and perverse generation which the Bible talks about. Those who entertain ideas of continuing in secret faith hesitate to take baptism. Those who avoid baptism are depriving themselves of one means of grace. When a person takes baptism he openly confesses his faith in the Lord and the Lord is pleased with it. The Holy Spirit further strengthens him.

Some regard baptism as a climactic experience in Christian life. Once a person receives baptism he is considered to be through with everything. That is why some leaders intentionally delay giving baptism to the aspirants. They teach people to become perfect before they take baptism. Perhaps they have in mind baptism of John the Baptist. Is such baptism 'believers' baptism'? In the Acts of the Apostles we find an incident at Ephesus where Paul enquires from the local disciples whether they had received the gift of the Holy Spirit. They tell him that they did not and shocked him by saying that they never knew that there is a person called the Holy Spirit. When he asked them they say that they received only 'John's Baptism'. It is a clear indication that they vowed to give up all sin. It was only repentance. Though they heard about Jesus, they never received the Gospel. What is the use of such repentance? Paul had to give them the Gospel of Jesus Christ. Then they believed and received the Gospel and were baptized in the name of Jesus. They received the Holy Spirit and spoke in tongues. (Ac. 19:1-6).

There are some who insist that baptism should be in the name of Jesus. They forget that the writer in Acts is using the name of Jesus only to contrast believers' baptism from John's baptism. Even when Peter talked about 'baptism in the name of Jesus,' on the day of Pentecost and also at Cornelius' house, it was only to emphasise the dawn of a new era. (Ac. 2:38). Jesus in the Great commission says that they should baptize in the name of the Father and of the Son and of the Holy Spirit. (Mt. 28:19). Those who want to walk according to the Spirit take baptism to openly confess their faith. They receive many blessings. They are initiated into a fellowship of God's children - the Church. They naturally join others in corporate worship.

Worship

"God is spirit, and his worshipers must worship in spirit and in truth." (Jn. 4:24).

Worship to God is offered by showing reverential fear and adoring awe and wonder. The Holy Spirit enables a believer to worship God in spirit and in truth. The emphasis in the Bible is more on congregational worship than on individual worship. Jesus went to the synagogue as it was His custom. His mother taught Him this custom from His childhood. But she always inculcated worship that is the love of the heart towards the Heavenly Father. Jesus learnt it from His childhood. He teaches that God is to be loved with all the mind, heart and strength. Mind, in all its ability to grasp His word and will, Heart with all its ability to show the Spirit controlled emotions and body in all its ability to serve God, should be engaged in worship. Accordingly Paul urges believers to offer their bodies as a living sacrifice. He calls this the spiritual act of worship. (Ro. 12:1).

Worshipping in spirit is walking according to the Spirit. The writer to the Hebrews calls it a sacrifice of praise - the fruit of the lips that confess His name. He exhorts the believers to keep meeting for worship. (Heb. 10:25; 13:15). In Hosea we find the promotion of this form of worship. (Hos. 14:2). We worship basically because we know who He is. God in his grace answers prayers and forgives sins. This causes the recipients to worship and praise Him. Besides words from the lips, musical instruments have a place in the worship. Early narratives in the Bible on prophesy strongly link prophesy with music. Prophet Samuel tells Saul that he will, on his way, meet a group of prophets coming in the company of musicians with various instruments. He adds saying that they will prophesy. (I Sa. 10:5). On a later day Samuel asks the kings of Israel and Judah who approach him for help from God, to call for a musician so that the hand of the Lord might come upon him. Then he gives God's word to them. The Psalmist exhorts people to worship God through song, music and dance. (Ps 96:1, 98:1, 150:3-6).

These days, Christian praise and worship sessions are drawing world attention. These gain access to millions. These have great potentiality to proclaim the Gospel. 'Praise and Worship' now is the catch word for Christian Fellowships. Times of David with his men at the ark of God are reappearing now. (II Sa. 6:5, 14). Then it was a time of celebration. We may say the Lord's resurrection and the coming of the Holy Spirit are to be celebrated now. True, but the Bible doesn't record any such commemoration in the early Church. Perhaps it was a delight of a different kind. There are some who quote from Psalm 98 and other portions to promote writing of new songs. New songs are released in the world on a scale unheard of before. But we should not forget that in their time a new song was a song which was to be subsequently incorporated into the Bible. There is always the danger of conforming ourselves to the world where love of music is at its peak now. New songs without God's word in the lyrics detract listeners from Biblical truth.

Simplicity was the key note of worship services in the house Churches, in Acts. These consisted for the most part praise, prayer, reading from the Scriptures and exposition. Paul says, 'Let the word of Christ dwell in you richly as you teach and admonish one another with all wisdom, and as you sing psalms, hymns and spiritual songs with gratitude in your hearts to God.' (Col. 3:16). Ecstasy - the feeling of intense delight is all right. It may lead us into dancing at times. There was celebration in music and dance in the presence of the father over the return of the prodigal son. We need to love God with all our heart. Heart is the seat of all emotions. But is that all? What about loving with our mind? Are we receiving substantial amount of exposition of God's word? Is there enough time for God's word in our 'Praise and Worship' sessions? After prolonged periods of singing, can there be alertness of mind for listening to God's word? In some cases - yes - in some cases may be - no. The concern here is that there should be a genuine response to the leading of the Holy Spirit in praise and worship. What about loving God with all our strength? Where are we spending our energy- the power of physical ability, which is seen in our intellect, influence, physical resources etc.? We need to have longing for witnessing to others. It is in going out and spending time with people in their daily life situations, we are supposed to be witnesses to Him.

Witness

"But you will receive power when the Holy Spirit comes on you; and you will be my witnesses in Jerusalem, and in all Judea and Samaria, and to the ends of the earth." (Ac. 1:8).

A witness is a person who has first-hand knowledge of an incident. Witnesses in the New Testament are those who testify to the fact of the death and resurrection of Jesus for salvation. The Holy Spirit empowers the believers to witness. It is because of the fact that the Holy Spirit is present in them, the disciples appeared to people as those who turned the world upside down. (Ac. 17:6). People recognised them as those who were with Jesus. (Ac. 4:13) What a transformation in individual lives! Christian victory is directly related to witnessing. (Rev. 12:11).

These days we hear preachers challenging the believers in the Fellowships to build their testimonies. This might be with a concern for the Fellowship. Their desire is to see that the Fellowship does not acquire a bad name because of individual bad witnesses. It is a natural reaction on the part of the leaders of the Fellowships as there are outsiders pointing fingers at the individual members. People may give an excuse, saying that the lives of the believers in the Fellowship are not good, when the leaders ask them to accept the Gospel. They should be told that Jesus never projected the lives of His disciples to make people believe in Him. The leaders are to build up faith and ethical behaviour in the individual lives of the believers, round the year, through the feeding of God's word. A witness is not the focal point for salvation. He is only a pointer to the cross. When the focus is turned from the cross and the resurrection to the life and witness of a believer, a wrong emphasis is made. Believers tend to make efforts to look good. No wonder they are being conformed to the likeness of their Fellowship than to the image of His Son! There are occasions when only testimonies are shared in public meetings. They might be tempted to present it to look effective. Further, there are some books to project experiences of individuals in the name of biographies. In so doing there is every possibility for being tempted by them to present their Christian getup or Christian mask. If Jesus hated anything the most, it is hypocrisy.

Further, the will of the Lord is to enable the believers, to be witnesses through the power of the Holy Spirit. It is primarily their being witnesses, that matters and not their acting as witnesses. However strongly we challenge the believers, it is of no avail until we learn to feed them with God's word. The Holy Spirit builds a believer by making him walk step by step in God's light. We cannot walk according to the Spirit if we suppress the Spirit who wants to enable us to witness. The early Church grew by leaps and bounds through witnessing. Witnessing is a way through which the power of the Holy Spirit is demonstrated. It is not a believer proving God but it is God who is proving Himself through the life and witness of a believer. Witnessing proceeds from the assurance of salvation and results in fellowship. John talks about the authenticity of the Gospel and their assurance of salvation. He says that they proclaim the word of Christ so that others may also have fellowship with them- the fellowship which they have with the Father and the Son. (I Jn. 1:1-3).

Fellowship

"If you have any encouragement from being united with Christ, if any comfort from his love, if any fellowship with the Spirit, if any tenderness and compassion…" (Php. 2:1).

Fellowship essentially is of the Spirit. Fellowship primarily refers to a believer's participation with others in something rather than to his association with others. It is basically, common sharing in direct spiritual realities. In Acts we see that the early believers spent time to have a share together. 'They devoted themselves to the apostles' teaching and to the fellowship, to the breaking of bread and to prayer.' 'All the believers were together and had everything in common.' (Ac. 2:42, 44). When we note that they had everything in common, it astonishes us greatly. But when God gave the Israelites Manna, each one was able to gather only what he needed. So in the early Church it was God's demonstration of what fellowship could be at its best.

John says that our fellowship is with the Father and with His Son. Paul says that we are heirs of God and co-heirs with Christ. So it is fellowship indeed! (Ro. 8:17). If assurance of salvation causes witnessing and if witnessing causes fellowship, what is all this for? It is to make the joy of the new entrant and all others, full. (I Jn. 1:4). How pure the motive is! It is not for adding numbers for strengthening the organization and its leadership but for the perfect joy of everybody.

Christian leaders are working day and night to build Fellowships. It is seen from experience that the more they are trying, the more they are failing. Fellowships are splitting and further splitting. Where does the defect lie? John gives us a clue. We note that there are three wrong claims we may be allowed to make in the Fellowships. First, we may claim that we have fellowship with God while we still walk in darkness. Secondly, we may claim that we are without sin and thirdly, we may claim that we have not sinned. There are some Fellowships formed exclusively to claim that they have no sin. John scores out all these claims. He gives only one way to build a Fellowship. It is by confessing our known sins and by walking in the light step by step for the cleansing of our unknown sins. It is like, all the believers standing in a circle with God's light at the centre. When everyone proceeds in the light towards the centre, they go closer and closer not only to God but also to one another and incidentally a strong Fellowship is built. (I Jn. 1:5-10). The central activity here is the 'Breaking of Bread.'

The Lord's Supper

"They all ate the same spiritual food." (I Co. 10:3).

The Lord's Supper if it is taken worthily it expresses itself in proclaiming the Lord's death until He comes. Paul says that we proclaim the Lord's death by taking the bread and wine. (I Co. 11:26). When the Israelites ate manna it was their spiritual food and when they drank from the rock it was spiritual drink. 'The Rock' was none other than

Christ. (I Co. 10:3, 4). God in His faithfulness nourished them and made them march forward to 'the Promised Land'.

Jesus asked them to eat the bread and drink the wine to remember Him. His broken body and his shed blood should always be in the focus for any believer. (Gal. 6:14). The more the number of times a believer shares in the 'Lord's Table' the greater is his remembrance of the Cross of Christ. His proclamation of Christ's death is all the more powerful. Walking in the spirit necessitates participation in the Lord's Table as it is a spiritual exercise.

The bread and wine are the mystery elements which a believer receives. Along with baptism this is a practice which is objectively seen. The mystery elements are to be taken reverentially. In the Corinthian Church exactly the opposite was happening. Paul was very much concerned about it. He says, 'In the following directives I have no praise for you, for your meetings do more harm than good.' (I Co. 11:17). Some Fellowships use this passage to instil fear in the minds of believers. It may make the believers to delay taking the Lord's Supper. Some skip it whenever they find themselves uneasy with themselves. Some pastors often quote some verses to disallow believers from participating in the Lord's Table. They say that whoever eats the bread or drinks the cup of the Lord in an unworthy manner will be guilty of sinning against the body and blood of the Lord. (I Co. 11:27, 32). But what does the word 'unworthy' mean in this context? The practice that time was, taking a Eucharistic Meal. Here 'unworthily' means eating the meal unmindful of others' need and ignoring the importance of 'doing it in remembrance of Him.' (I Co. 11:23-26). Further, let us note that personal confessing and receiving cleansing is an everyday affair- not just when we approach the Table. We approach it to become more focussed on the Cross of Christ. We prepare ourselves to proclaim the Gospel. The Holy Spirit equips us with spiritual gits to proclaim our Lord's death. We wait in the presence of the Lord to know our gift so that we serve Him effectively.

Spiritual gifts

"All these are the work of one and the same Spirit, and he gives them to each one, just as he determines." (I Co. 12:11).

God's people are to be prepared for works of service. The body of Christ is to be built up. Unity of faith and knowledge of the Son of God are to be reached. Maturity and fullness of Christ are to be attained. Paul says, 'It was he who gave some to be apostles, some to be prophets, some to be evangelists, and some to be pastors and teachers, to prepare God's people for works of service, so that the body of Christ may be built up until we all reach unity in the faith and in the knowledge of the Son of God and become mature, attaining to the whole measure of the fullness of Christ.' (Eph. 4:11-13). The Holy Spirit endows each one with a gift. 'Now to each one the manifestation of the Spirit is given for the common good. To one there is given through the Spirit the message of wisdom, to another the message of knowledge by means of the same Spirit, to another faith by the same Spirit, to another gifts of healing by that one Spirit, to another miraculous powers, to another prophecy, to another distinguishing between spirits, to another speaking in different kinds of tongues, and to still another the interpretation of tongues. All these are the work of one and the same Spirit, and he gives them to each one, just as he determines.' (I Co. 12:7-11). These gifts and gifts recorded elsewhere could be categorised as gifts of utterance and gifts for practical service. Gifts of utterance are apostleship, prophecy, teaching and tongues. An apostle proclaims the gospel to the unbelieving world, a prophet conveys divine revelations of temporary significance to edify, a teacher expounds the established doctrine and a person speaking in tongues edifies when all that he speaks is interpreted.

Gifts for practical service can be categorised as gifts of power, gifts of sympathy and gifts of administration. Working wonders, miracles and healings come under gifts of power. Helping, liberal alms giving and works of mercy come under gifts of sympathy while governing authority possessed by ruling elders could be called gift of administration. Some gifts look natural while other gifts look supernatural. Whether natural or supernatural, these gifts are to be invested like talents. Jesus sends out seventy others to every town ahead of Him. They return rejoicing and saying, "Lord, even the demons submit to us in your name." Even today, when our gifts are exercised it gives us great delight. We may be tempted to take the glory for ourselves. Even if we do not take the glory we need to be mindful that it is for the good of others. So far as our benefit is concerned it is joy centred on the fact of our being. The Lord tells the seventy: 'However, do not rejoice that the spirits submit to you, but rejoice that your names are written in heaven.' (Lk. 10:20). Those who walk in the Spirit rejoice in knowing who they are. They recognise their gifts and employ their gifts for the extension of Christ's kingdom.

Conclusion

Jesus promised His disciples the Spirit of truth. He equated the presence of the Spirit with that of the presence of the Father and the Son in the life of a believer. He told His disciples that the Holy Spirit will live with them and will be in them. He added that the Holy Spirit will guide them into all truth. (Jn. 14:16, 17, 23; 16:13). The writers of the Epistles, inspired by the Holy Spirit, showed various means of grace. Tapping His grace through these is exactly what walking in the Spirit is all about. The Spirit, dwelling in us, leads us to all means of grace which God the Father made available to us. This is a daily walk. No wonder Paul concludes his teaching on 'walking in the Spirit' saying, 'since we live by the Spirit, let us keep in step with the Spirit.' (Gal. 5:25). This means that the Holy Spirit is ahead of us paving the way for us to receive His grace through the Scripture, prayer, baptism, worship, witness, fellowship, the Lord's Supper and spiritual gifts for our strength. He is involved in each one of these, helping us to walk step by step. It is a systematic walk round the clock along with Him, as we belong to Him, all the time, whether we are awake or asleep.

CHAPTER VI

Armour – Six fold

Paul exhorts the believers to be strong in the Lord and in His mighty power. He foresees the direct role of the enemy. The enemy tries in various ways to weaken the faith life of a believer. This is particularly true when a believer takes a step forward. In the Spiritual walk we march against the true enemy who is behind the flesh and blood. He is the ruler of the forces of evil who is none other than Satan. (Eph.2:2). Paul says in the sixth chapter of Ephesians that we should put on the full armour of God so that we can take our stand against his schemes. He talks about these in the particular context of the interpersonal relationships of the believers. Paul talks about the six fold armour, to present the spiritual truth. The armour is seen from Paul's time through the centuries till today, in various forms. In it, each piece has its specific use and it stands along with all other pieces in its importance. It has its purposefulness only when it is together with the rest. (Eph. 6:10-18).

The Girdle – the belt of truth buckled around the waist

The belt a man buckles around his waist keeps him fit. The Bible truth is of great importance in the life of a believer. This truth is opposed to falsehood. The Bible itself is the truth. The believer, who begins with simple faith, should continue to engage himself with this truth in his every day practical life. For this, understanding the Bible, as a whole, is a necessity. Sound Christian doctrine is to be possessed by him. He takes care of having it soon after he entertains the thought of standing firm. Paul uses the girdle as symbol for truth. Dependability, consistency and reliability show the truth in a person. Reliability is basically an attribute of God. (Ps 31:5). The Bible reveals the character of God. Jesus says that God's word is the truth. (Jn. 17:17). In the final analysis, the believer has in him, Jesus, the personification of truth. (Jn. 14:6). This truth is to be seen in his interpersonal relationships.

The Breastplate – the righteousness wrapped around the chest

Right action and fair dealing are to be seen in our interpersonal relationships. (Am. 5:24; Mi. 6:8). When Paul talks about the righteousness of God in contrast to the righteousness of the Law, he points to its source. The source of righteousness is God. But how can man approach God to obtain this? Man should be righteous to relate himself with God. Man by himself cannot reach the standard of God's righteousness. The believer through the gospel possesses the right relationship with God. God justified him on the basis of the righteousness of His Son. The believer, now, continues to hunger for this righteousness. Jesus promises that he will be filled. (Mt 5:5). Now, it is the righteousness of Christ which is deposited in him. (I Co. 1:30). It should be brought out in his every day practical living. These days attacks of Satan are in the area of a believer's 'relationships'. There is a breakdown of relationships both in the family and in the society. A believer can guard his family and the Fellowship and his community by drawing out the righteousness of Jesus, present in him.

The Brazen boots – readiness that comes from the Gospel of peace

There is only one way for participating in the expansion, in the kingdom of God. That is by preaching the Gospel. If the devil succeeds in closing the mouth of the believer half the battle is won for him. Christian discipleship is not only in being with the Master but it is also in being sent by Him to preach the Good News in His power. It is an alternating experience. The great commission of Christ is to preach the Gospel to all the people. The believer should always be ready with this Gospel of peace. Paul quotes from the O.T. to mention about the beauty of the feet of such men. The number of such men these days is dwindling. The statement, "your actions speak louder than your words" make us infer that the preacher's genuineness is being doubted. Satan is behind causing such doubts. There is no alternative to the Gospel. It is "euangelion"- Good News which is to be proclaimed by mouth. The preacher should go on, only being mindful of his actions.

The Shield – taking up faith which extinguishes the flaming arrows

The idea of faith is conveyed by the words "believe", "trust" or "hope". It is in the faithfulness of God a believer puts his trust. In a way it is rationalistic as this is trust in the trustworthy character of God. Creating doubt in the believers on the faithfulness of God and His ability to help and lead, is an arrow in the quiver of the enemy. In the Garden of Eden the very first arrow that he employed was doubt on God's word. The initial faith which leads the believer into the kingdom of God is on the finished work of Christ. 'The faith', which Paul now is, talking about, is the continuing attitude of trust in that work. Paul adds, only with regard to this piece, a word on the benefit it bestows. He says that it extinguishes all the flaming arrows of the evil one. The believer needs to make sure that he protects himself before he advances into the enemy's territory. Faith alone protects him. This is to be guarded. This defends him from all the attacks of the evil one. God's word nourishes this faith (Ro. 10:17)

The Helmet – holding the cup of salvation

Salvation is the greatest gift a believer receives from God. It includes everything which the believer needs – forgiveness of sins, health, protection, prosperity etc. – the key factor being the forgiveness of sins. When Paul says that God has given the Holy Spirit he does not speak of some special experience. (Ro 5:5). He says that the Holy Spirit witnesses within the believer that he is a child of God. (Ro 8:16). We can infer from his statement that the unshakable assurance of salvation and son ship, a believer has, is the evidence of the presence of the Holy Spirit. He gives this as the only evidence of the indwelling of the Holy Spirit. It is logical to think that Paul takes these as natural results of "Justification" a believer receives. A believer should have the assurance of salvation. Any doubt on his salvation is fatal. The experience of salvation is to be treasured by the believer. His mind should be gripped by the fact of the salvation which he possesses now. He should also be conscious of the fact that he is being saved progressively from the power of sin and that he can hope to be saved from the very presence of sin prospectively. His present life should be a life of celebration and thankfulness to the Lord. He is to worship the Lord holding the cup of salvation.

The Sword – taking the word of God

For a believer, while all other pieces of the armour are for defending himself, this piece is for attacking the enemy. Jesus defeated the enemy when he was tempted, only by quoting the written word of God. In the book of Revelation Jesus is called the "Faithful and True". His name is "the Word of God". On his thigh, His name is written as the "King of kings and Lord of Lords". A sharp sword comes out of His mouth. He rules the nations with an iron sceptre. (Rev 19:11-16). The sharp sword which comes out of His mouth is the decider of all. Paul uses the symbol of the sword for the word of God. The imagery presented in the book of Revelation can make us say that this sword should come out of the mouth of a believer. Paul speaks about confessing with our mouth. (Ro 10:9). This confession gives the believer the due victory. (Rev 12:11). Paul asks the Colossians to allow the word of Christ to richly dwell in them while they teach and admonish one another. The believer can march forward to possess the territory by speaking out the written word of God.

Conclusion

Truth, righteousness, readiness for the gospel, faith, salvation and the word of God are all equally important. The over emphasis of one of the pieces of armour over all other pieces is the final trick of Satan to make us defenceless. Any preaching which offers only one of these and over simplifies the believer's spiritual battle is done under the influence of Satan. Such preaching weakens the believer and makes him vulnerable to the attacks of the evil one. Paul asks the Ephesian believers to pray in the Sprit on all occasions so that they can be alert in using the full armour of God. Prayer to Paul is the binding force that keeps all pieces of armour in their proper place. The battle, according to him is not to be fought alone. The believer should know that the saints along with the believer are in the battle. The believers are to pray for one another so that they can fight unitedly, putting on the full armour of God. The whole battle can be seen as the kingdom of God advancing and possessing the enemy's territory.

CHAPTER VII

The Journey ahead

Now, you are able to identify some of the winds of teaching which toss you to and fro. You also know that you do not need to be blown here and there by every wind of teaching. You have noted the principles of understanding your Bible; you do not want to compromise on the essential doctrines; you want to take fully the truth present in pairs and you want to welcome experiences of all kinds and all means of grace present in the Bible and you want to put on the full armour of God and you want to pray in the Spirit on all occasions. Now, you know that you belong to the New Covenant. The Holy Spirit indwells you. Paul says that you have an obligation to live by the Spirit as you have received the Spirit of His Son. You need to voluntarily stretch out to slip your hand into the hand of the Holy Spirit. The deposit of sound teaching is the only tool you can employ to detect false teaching. (II Ti. 1:14). You have sound teaching in you to enable you to detect false teaching and stay away from it. Paul says that there are some who have rejected sound teaching and so have shipwrecked their faith. You need to sail safe in the light of such possibility.

The enemy is waiting

The devil is very much at work in the world. To those who haven't begun their faith life at all, he tells them that they had begun. To those who had just begun, he tells them that they have already arrived. To those who are walking in faith, he tells them that they can walk the way they think is the best. He doesn't allow people to come to the knowledge of truth. However, if they turn him down and receive the Gospel, he devises various ways of wasting their time. Peter says that the enemy, the devil prowls around like a roaring lion looking for someone to devour. (I Pe. 5:6-9). You have to be alert to foil the plans of the devil. James says that the devil will flee away if we submit to God and resist him. Long time ago, when our elder son, at the age of two, tried to chase a cat, an interesting thing happened. Initially it tried to run away when he chased it. But sensing no threat, it stopped. Our son also stopped. Picking up courage, it turned towards him. Then our son started running back to us screaming. The devil is like that. He scares us if we are afraid of him. He will chase us when we choose to run. If we stand as the cat does, he too stands. If we chase him, he runs away from us.

Stand firm - you are called

You have received God's calling. You have accepted Jesus as your saviour. Others may say that they are not called. Long time ago I was returning from college after work. A former student of the college greeted me. I stopped my bicycle and asked him, to find out from him, when he would be marrying. He stared at me for a while and said, "Sir, I gave you my wedding invitation last summer". I felt ashamed. Why did I not remember? Might be I turned down the invitation the very moment he gave it to me. Was I not invited? Yes, I was. Why did I not remember? It is because, I rejected it straight away. Had I attended, witnessed the wedding and took part in the wedding dinner, I would not have put such a silly question to him. Those who say that they are not called by God, perhaps, come under this category.

You have a glorious hope. Paul states, 'I pray also that the eyes of your heart may be enlightened in order that you may know the hope to which he has called you, the riches of his glorious inheritance in the saints.' (Eph. 1:18). For this you need to stand firm in faith. For this you have to be sure of your salvation. You can trust His word. Jesus says, 'I tell you the truth, whoever hears my word and believes him who sent me has eternal life and will not be condemned; he has crossed over from death to life.' (Jn. 5:24). John says, concerning those who believed, 'I write these things to you who believe in the name of the Son of God so that you may know that you have eternal life.' (I Jn. 5:13). God doesn't lie. So you can be sure of your salvation. Jesus says that devil is a liar and the father of lies. He creates doubts. Do not entertain doubts about your salvation.

Paul says, 'As a prisoner for the Lord, then, I urge you to live a life worthy of the calling you have received.' (Eph. 4:1). Life worthy of His calling is to be characterised by humility. It is the character of the Lord. You need to long for humility. Paul concludes his teaching on walking in the Spirit by saying, 'Let us not become conceited, provoking and envying each other.' (Gal. 5:26). The greatest hurdle in interpersonal relationships is conceit. The devil tickles our ego. The greatest threat to Christianity is from within. The devil knows fully well that egotistic men can fight fierce battles in the Church among themselves. So Paul exhorts, 'Be completely humble and gentle; be patient, bearing with one another in love.' (Eph. 4:2). How tragic it is if we fight among ourselves in spite of the fact that the same Spirit indwells all the believers! We need to have love to overcome infighting.

Love - the key to unity

God is love. This characteristic of God is made available to believers. This love is to be released in interpersonal relationships. Jesus demonstrated this in His interpersonal relationships. He did not compromise truth while showing His love. He was generous in complimenting when anyone deserved. He never hesitated to condemn when anyone did anything wrong. There was never a prejudicial statement against any one. Instead there was unconditional love for all those whom He met. You need to grow along these lines finally to show unconditional love. This makes you keep the unity of the Spirit through the bond of peace and keeps you in a warm fellowship.

Unity - the key to service

The Holy Spirit is there to help. We need to learn to lean on Him. He is the one who causes us to show love and to have unity. The fact of the matter is that the whole work of God is in Unity. Paul says, 'There is one body and one Spirit- just as you were called to one hope when you were called- one Lord, one faith, one baptism; one God and Father of all, who is over all and through all and in all. But to each one of us grace has been given as Christ apportioned it.' (Eph. 4:4-7). Your job is to be watchful to see whether you are staying in or falling out from the unity of faith. This enables you to serve others according to grace that is apportioned to you.

Service – the key to maturity

God's people are to be prepared for God's work. God has a plan for building His Church- the body of Christ. His Church now is the kingdom of God in miniature. The Holy Spirit bestows gifts which equip others to serve the Church by exercising their gifts. You are serving others and others are serving you. In this process Christian maturity is becoming possible. Paul says, 'His intent was that now, through the church, the manifold wisdom of God should be made known to the rulers and authorities in the heavenly realms.' (Eph. 3:10). Now you know that as a member of the Church, you are in God's grand plan. You keep going. You don't need to be afraid. You have life support. It is faith addressed to faith. (Ro. 1:17). Faith comes from hearing the word of Christ. (Ro. 10:17). So you have God's word to fall back on, all along your sail. It is a journey from God's word to God's word until you are transformed into the image of His Son.

Conclusion of the matter - from God's word to God's word!

You have a lesson from the Berean believers. They received the message with great eagerness from Paul. But they did not take his teaching for granted. They examined the Scriptures after returning each day, to see if what Paul said was true. For Peter, God's word is more important than his experience on the mount of transfiguration! (II Pe.

1:16-21). You need to keep yourself open to God's word. 'All Scripture is God-breathed and is useful for teaching, rebuking, correcting and training in righteousness, so that the man of God may be thoroughly equipped for every good work.' (II Ti. 3:16, 17).

How privileged you are to have the Bible in your hands. Roman emperor Diocletian wanted to annihilate the Bible. He sent his army to do away with it. He is gone and his army is gone but the Bible remains. It says,'..., "All men are like grass, and all their glory is like the flowers of the field the grass withers and the flowers fall, but the word of the Lord stands forever." And this is the word that was preached to you' (I Pe. 1:24, 25). Further, Heads of institutions with vested interests wanted to confine the Bible for themselves. But God delivered it from their hands to pass it on to you. Translations were hindered in the name of sanctity. But God arranged for translating His word into your language. It is handed down intact from cover to cover. All that you need is to have a fresh look at it to make it your own - a fresh look to observe, interpret and apply.

In the pages of the Bible we find God's progressive revelation. The Old Testament is the foundation on which the super structure, the New Testament, is built. In the Old Testament we find prophesy while in the New Testament we find its fulfilment. Only when they saw Jesus, the disciples understood that Jesus is the Second Person in the Godhead. Only when Jesus returned to the Father and when the Holy Spirit came, the disciples understood that there is the Third Person in the Holy Trinity. All teachings on God based only on the Old Testament are bound to be erroneous.

There is so much of narration in the Bible. Gospels contain incidents. Acts of the Apostles also contain incidents concerning the acts of the Holy Spirit through the Apostles. Observation of these is very much necessary. But all teachings based on incidents in the New Testament without reference to teaching in the epistles are bound to be erroneous. Such teachings do not stand the test of overall understanding of the Scripture.

The writers of the epistles were granted revelation to interpret the incidents. Paul talks about it. 'Although I am less than the least of all God's people, this grace was given me: to preach to the Gentiles the unsearchable riches of Christ, and to make plain to everyone the administration of this mystery, which for ages past was kept hidden in God, who created all things.' (Eph. 3:8, 9). The writers of the epistles have an overall understanding of the theological purpose of the Scriptures as the Holy Spirit led them to all truth. The doctrines presented in the light of such understanding are with genuine intentions. They lead believers to unity of faith. Paul's teaching on salvation, Christian life and ministry offers insight into the Scripture to enable us to apply it to ourselves. (Ro. 16:25-27).

If the insight is accepted and received we will no longer be infants. We will be matured men and women in Christ. Paul says, 'Then we will no longer be infants, tossed back and forth by the waves, and blown here and there by every wind of teaching and by the cunning and craftiness of men in their deceitful scheming. Instead, speaking the truth in love, we will in all things grow up into him who is the Head, that is, Christ.' (Eph. 4:14, 15).

We, now, know that all things God works for our good. What good is this to us excepting in the final analysis our being conformed to the likeness of His son, the first born? Who are we if Jesus is the first born? We are God's children - brothers and sisters of Jesus Christ. Who else has the right to be like Him excepting you and I? 'Likeness of His Son' is sure to result in you and in me. There is hope for us to be conformed into His image. It is because we are in God's love. John says, 'How great the love is, the Father has lavished on us, that we should be called children of God! And that is what we are! The reason the world does not know us is that it did not know him. Dear friends, now we are children of God, and what we will be has not yet been made known. But we know that when he appears, we shall be like him, for we shall see him as he is. Everyone who has this hope in him purifies himself, just as he is pure.' (I Jn. 3:1-3). Holding on to this hope, let us walk in the light.

Printed in the United States
By Bookmasters